The Last Crawl

By

Christopher Slevin

Copyright © 2024 by Christopher Slevin
All rights reserved.
Hardcover ISBN: 9798326352392
Paperback ISBN: 9798328016865

No part of this publication may be reproduced, distributed, or transmitted in any form or by any means, including photocopying, recording, or other electronic or mechanical methods, without the prior written permission of the publisher, except as permitted by copyright law. For permission requests, contact [include publisher / author contact info].

The story, all names, characters, and incidents portrayed in this production are fictitious. No identification with actual persons (living or deceased), places, buildings, and products is intended or should be inferred.

Book Cover photo by: pixabay.com/focal_leat-19740/
1st edition 2024

Lyrics referenced in the book:
"Mister Writer" lyrics copyright Kelly Jones and Marshall Bird
"I Fall to Pieces" lyrics copyright Hank Cochran and Harlan Howard
'Unchained Melody' lyrics copyright Hy Zaret

For Olivia and Finn, as always

"Life is too short to read a bad book."
— **James Joyce**

"Some books are so familiar that reading them is like being home again."
— **Louisa May Alcott**

"Nobody reads anymore"
— *David Dowling*

PROLOGUE:

The phone buzzes beside my ear. I'm lying on the couch, frantically searching for the source of the vibration. I pull me phone out from under a cushion and glance at the name before tapping the green button. It's Kevin.

'What's the craic?'

– 'Story,' he says. There is a pause. His words travel across a sea of stars before reaching my ear. 'Yeah, listen, he's dying... I think you should come back.'

Straight to the point.

'Fuck.'

–'Yeah,' he says.

'I'll look up flights,' I say.

–'Have you been drinking?'

Again, straight to the point.

'It's half ten in the evening.'

–'It's Monday.'

Now, it's my turn to pause.

'I'll look up flights,' I say.

PROLOGUE MARK II:

If this were a Richard Curtis movie, I would start it with something like;

Dear diary in my head, you were right; it does suck being an adult. It's fucking gratuitous. Not only do I have to fly back to Ireland for me Da's funeral— if he does end up dying this time, I have to pay a king's ransom to get there. I'd blame COVID-19 on it but the greedy bastards that run the airlines only hike up the prices of flights for their Christmas bonuses. They say there's no one to run the airports, so the cost of travel has increased to reduce the number of fuckers like me coming through.

If this were like that Christmas movie he made, I'd meet a girl at the gate, you know– the one. She's business-savvy and has two kids. I'm the lonely writer heading home to his poor Da's funeral. She'd be tapping on her phone, getting the last bit of work in before that trip to Ireland to meet her boss, who'll end up trying to seduce her. I'll be the number on her phone that she calls when she's down in the dumps. We'll end up…

Ah, who am I kidding? This is no romcom movie. It's not even a movie of the week. If you saw this story on TV, you'd switch the channel. This story deserves to sit on a shelf in an airport, constantly getting looked at but not bought. Who'd want to read a story about a man returning to Ireland to his dying Da? Sounds fucking depressing. No one wants to read about an alcoholic know-it-all who endures his family for a few days while learning a secret that should have been obvious from the start. No, they don't. You don't. So put this down and pick up that copy of Good Night Stories for Rebel Girls. That's a class book.

1

I get a call while at the airport bar, glancing at the board. I've been waiting the last half an hour for "*Go To Gate*" to change to "*Boarding*". I look at the phone display. It's Ma. I clear my throat and think all things sober.

'Hi, Ma.'

'David! Great, you haven't boarded.'

'No, not for another—'

—'Listen, I was talking with your brothers, and I think— well, they think it would be a good idea for you to do the eulogy.'

'Ma! He's not even dead, yet.'

–'You have to prepare for these things,' she says earnestly. 'These things happen so fast.'

'No thanks.'

–'Grand, that's sorted.'

'Mam, I said "no".'

–'No– you said no thanks but you always do this. You say no, then I get one of your brothers to do it, you think they're doing a crap job, and you end up doing it anyway.'

'Not this time. I respectfully decline.'

–'Respectfully decline?'

'Yep.'

There is air on the phone, which is worrying because my mother could talk for the Republic and the six counties in the North, too.

'Fine. I'll get Kevin to do it,' she finally says.

She says her goodbyes and hangs up. I'll order a cheeky pint. That's when I get a text. It's Kevin: *Don't be drunk when you get in.*

Me and Kevin have a relationship built on eggshells strategically placed on an active minefield. Him being the eldest with a superiority complex. Me being the youngest and the first in the family to actually do something with his life. He never forgave me for that.

I wanted to do the James Joyce thing and move somewhere foreign to write my masterpiece. He wanted me to help take some of my father's blows (both mentally and physically). He ended up being socially disabled, living across the street from my parent's house.

Me? I travelled Europe, moving from city to village to the next big city. I finally settled in Budapest with a crazy ex-girlfriend and a new book that has me banned from entering Turkey. (That last statement might be an exaggeration, but the Turks are not happy with me.)

Paul, the other brother, has middle-child syndrome. He tries too hard, takes the biggest swings and has the most spectacular falls. He's lost so much money in investments that didn't "quite pan out". He had money stolen from him by cowboys, who were his "partners". You get a picture of who he is.

My phone vibrates as I finally board the plane, I know it's him–Paul —- and I know exactly what it says: *We need to talk*. If I were to do a quick translation of Paul's language, it would mean: *"I need another loan on the loan that you've already lent me, which I've neglected to pay back."*

I ignore it.

I remember the days when you could choose your seat for free on a plane. Not anymore. I pay the extra fee to be seated in the first row. This way I have leg room, a short distance to the toilet and I'm within earshot from the flight attendants and their stash of beer.

***

The kind flight attendant named Robert gives me a beer mid-flight, and as soon as I crack the seal of the can, I begin to think about Da. I wish I didn't. He'll wreck me buzz.

Da was Da. An abuser in every sense. The poster boy for toxic masculinity. He reeked of it—that and alcohol. I guess I got that gene from him. The alcohol part. Not the abuse. I don't think I've ever been in a fight. Wait. No. That's a lie. There was that one time, but I don't want to get into that right now. Maybe later when I'm drunk.

I have the alcohol part under control. I think. I know when I'm drunk, and I stop drinking…. sometimes. I become funny and loose under the influence. Alcohol turned me Da into a thunderous cunt.

He is the beginning and end of this story. The reason for it to start and the means to an end… and I hate him for it.

I also hate the fact that I'm hovering over the lights that make up Dublin City, on his terms. It's killing me, justifying its beauty as we swing over Howth and into Swords, not because I want to come back, but because it was demanded of me. I can't wait to see the signs that greet me on my journey to the airport's exit. The ones that tell me I'm Irish without telling me I'm Irish. The slogans that plaster the long, unjustified trek to baggage. Those slogans that baffle the ordinary tourist who stumbled into the big smoke via Google-cheap-flights: *"The shinbone is the GPS to tell you where the furniture is"* or *"The pollen count, that's a difficult job"*.

I want to return on my own terms, not on his. I want to surprise me Ma with a TikTok-influenced post to gain some thousand-plus followers—the ones where you add a legend: *Wait until the end. You'll never guess her reaction.*

We touch down with a bounce and a pull. The engines roar like a hot laptop. I feel my pulse throb in my neck. My stomach aches from the lack of food and several beers. I smile at Robert, the flight attendant, as I disembark and make my way to the exit.

The fucking slogans are gone! Why would they take them down?

I thank the passport control officer when he says, 'Welcome home!'

I go out the door anticipating seeing a family member for a lift.

There is no one waiting.

My heart sinks. A woman's eyes light up when she sees me. A redhead in a brown leather jacket. She quickly looks away. I must look like someone she knows. No one I know here to pick me up.

I call Kevin because Ma never answers her phone.

'We were summoned to the hospital,' he says on the phone.

There is no point arguing now. I just ask where they are and take an expensive taxi ride to Blanchardstown.

***

Another thing I love about Dublin is that the taxi drivers give you great material for characters if you are a writer. My driver is a butch-looking lesbian whose pronouns are they/them and who hid their sexual preference from their mother until her deathbed. The mother knew all along but wanted to keep it a secret from the neighbours. I got all this info before we even left the airport. Anyway, here's a fun fact: They are the chief executive officer of the Pride Parade Organisation Office in the North Dublin section.

'That's a mouth full,' I tell them.

'That's our slogan,' they say. 'It's A Mouthful!'

We both have a giggle at that.

'Are yeh living abroad, are yeh?' they ask.

'How'd yeh guess?'

'You came out of the airport with a backpack and not the usual twenty kilo case.'

'You could be a detective.'

'Me ex was. Horrible bitch of a woman but sure-look-it, what can you do.'

When they ask me why I'm heading to Blanch Hospital from the airport, I tell them. They already have a feeling but want to ask anyway. They then add, 'Losing a parent is something every kid knows they have to deal with but is never ready for.'

This sentiment almost has me welling up.

Almost.

Remember, my Da was a cunt. A Grade-A-Certifiable-Thunder-Cunt, to be exact.

The taxi driver pulls up to the geriatric ward and lets me out.

'How much do I owe you?' I ask.

'Ah, sure, you can give me a hug and call it quits.'

I hug them awkwardly through the driver's window, and they say, 'I'm sorry for your troubles.'

This time, tears well up in my eyes. That statement suddenly hits on a different frequency now that I'm not saying it to the bereaved. This stranger is sorry for the troubles I'm going through, and I realise it will be the end of my troubles as soon as they are gone. 37 years of troubles. They should be handing out medals at the funeral.

***

The geriatric ward in Blanchardstown is way up the back from the main hospital—isolated, dark, and sombre. The glow of the lights from the entrance should be comforting; however, the jaundiced tint makes me feel sickly.

I drag my feet up the driveway and spot Kevin.

Fuck.

He stands just inside the door, his arms folded, trying to look important. He looks more like a doorman than a visitor. He catches my eye as I reach for the door handle. The look he gives me– the prick.

Are those tears?

'You made it,' he says and runs a finger across the corner of his eye.

Christ, I hate hospitals. They always have that smell. It's like burned plastic on a scientific level—that and disinfectant.

'No thanks to you bunch of pricks,' dig number one released into the wild. 'Left at the airport, I was –why are you crying?'

'In case you didn't notice, our Da is dying.'

'Yeah, but why are you crying?' I'm not known for giving low blows, but considering the circumstances.

–'Have you been drinking?'

'Do you only know the one tune, Kevin? This "have you been drinking" thing is boring, Kevin.' I added the second "Kevin" to invoke thoughts of Ma calling us by name when she was annoyed.

–'Yeah, it is…David. Maybe you should change the record so I won't have to point it out.'

Good shot. Stung a little but fuck it, I shall not get angry at this prick.

'So, where is the cunt?' I say, making sure I make eye contact. See, I can disconnect myself from him– me Da. I can call him the big

C and let the word hang out there, as it should, for shock value. It's the only word I can use in my arsenal to pierce any armour that my family decides to wear at any given moment. Saying it in the presence of Kevin makes it hit home. He's offended.

'You *have* been drinking,' he spits. 'And you want to go in a room with Ma like that?'

– 'Oh fuck off. Yes, I have been fucking drinking and talking to you makes me want to drink some more. A whole lot more. A shit ton more. Get langered, hammered, gee-eyed. So can we please see this cunt so I can get on with my journey finding a Guinness with the shtick that lasts till the end of the glass!'

'Don't call your father that.' Ma's voice shuts me right the fuck up.

I pivot, one eye closed, waiting for a clip around the ear. Nothing. She's in a black jumper and a black skirt. Jaysus, she shrunk. She walks up to me with gentle arms open.

'Sorry, Ma,' I say. Half-meaning it.

Kevin shakes his head like something from an amateur play. Ma ignores it. She looks me dead in the eye. Her eyes are small, cold, and worn. Mine are trying not to well up again. She has gotten so old since I last saw her.

Ma sinks into my chest.

'He is the big C, but we don't use those street words round here,' she whispers into my jacket. 'That's not the Dowling way.' She cranes her neck to look at me. Her tiny arms try to reach around my torso, giving me a cheeky smile and a squeeze. That's not the

Dowling way? My vernacular comes straight from the Dowling kitchen table on Sunday afternoons when me aunts came around for their weekly chat.

'C'mon,' Ma says.

She beckons me to the last room on the right at the end of an endlessly long corridor. All the doors are open, so nurses can have a peek in as they pass. That's my guess, anyway. It could also be to reassure the patients that they are not alone. My eye catches one older woman who lights up for a split second; then her eyes glaze over again. For that millisecond, I am someone that she knew. I am a son or a husband, an old boyfriend she has not seen since she was sixteen. I could have, God forbid, been a priest to her.

Just before I enter the last room me Da might ever see, a thought crosses my mind: everyone in these rooms will eventually die. I am surrounded by death. Maybe that's why everything smells of some sort of sanitiser? Death has a particular scent, and disinfectant would mask it. Again, that's my guess. However, when Ma opens the door to Da's room, I can almost smell death. Maybe the Grim Reaper smells of burnt plastic and disinfectant.

***

I remember the last time I saw him... me Da. Before today, I mean. I had just won the Booker Prize for *Cheers! Darling* and flew into Dublin for an overnight stay. I had planned just to meet Ma at the Gresham Hotel and give her me award. (I've been doing that since my first short story, *Winner*, back when I was sixteen.)

Anyway, I came down to the resident's bar and guess who was there with her? The big man himself. He made fun of me staying in "a fancy hotel" and drank several pints of Guinness without trying to strike up a decent conversation. I barely looked at him. I concentrated on me Ma and her news. Then it finally came out.

'Is there prize money with that trophy?'

I knew he was there for something. I told him there was, and all of a sudden, his attitude changed. He wanted to know about my life and how my next book was coming. He was ready to squeeze that money lemon. I didn't give in. I kept my money. Before he left, he called me a miserable cunt. That was the last time I saw him.

***

The person that lies in bed before me is not my Da. He looks nothing like him. I look at Ma, hoping she'd say, "Gotcha," but she gives me that look. The "I know" look.

'Don't be frightened. He hasn't been himself for the last few months. Just withering away.'

Fucking hell!

You have to understand, my Da was a tank of a man. He was tall and broad with huge, digger-hands. This thing in the bed was a shell. His cheekbones stuck out like someone had sucked all the air out of Angelina Jolie. His skin looked like modelling plastic. His eyes– Jaysus, his eyes. They were fixed to the top right-hand corner of the room. Like he was staring at the unseen Grim Reaper, and death was like, *'Nah, suffer some more.'*

He *was* suffering. I could see that. His breath was shallow and too far apart for any normal man. His jaw was locked, so it looked like he sang all the "Ahs" in a choir.

'Ah!' a voice said, as if someone was reading my mind. 'You must be the other son.'

A male nurse stood behind me. Asian. I don't want to pick a region– that might make me racist.

Does me calling him Asian make me a racist anyway, by generalisation?

Anyway, he was bald with glasses that made him look like every other hard-working nurse that strained their fucking eyes reading textbook after textbook so they could change geriatric nappies.

'How'a'ya,' I said, stepping away from the bed.

He fed me Da a syringe full of clear liquid. When he pulled up the hospital blankets for that moment, I could see how skinny Da was. I don't think he'd even class as a paperweight at this stage. The nurse smiled awkwardly and returned to plunge the syringe into a box that controlled the medicine intake.

'What is that?' I ask.

'Morphine.'

–'Oh…'

I knew what that meant.

    'Just to make him comfortable,' the nurse said.

–'Hm…'

'I'll give you a moment.' And the nurse left.

Ma put an arm on my shoulder. 'I'll give you a minute too.'

She took a step to leave, but I reached for her hand. She took it briefly and nodded to let me know I got this. Then she left me alone with him.

Fuck.

Double fuck.

I can't look at him.

His nose looks enormous. Did he always have a big nose?

I can't look at him.

What was he staring at? If I look at the corner long enough, will I see it too?

He gurgles. I freak out. Was he dying? Right now?

No, wait. It must have been the morphine kicking in.

I calm my shit down and pace the floor.

I can't look at him.

Why were those tears coming back? He was a horrible Grade-A-thunder cun–

'Day-vvid.'

I look at him. There was no way his lungs had enough juice to produce that sound. I wait for the longest time to see his frail chest rise again. He gasps for air like someone waking abruptly from a deep sleep. Then there is nothing. I move closer to his mouth, a trick I learned at a first-aid course. Stick your ear to the patient's mouth and stare at their chest. My ear was over his mouth, and I'm looking for signs of movement on his chest. Jaysus, his breath stinks.

I wait. Panic wants to come out to play because that nightgown was not moving.

I wait even longer.

Fuck.

Should I call for help or–

There is something different on his face. His eyes are not looking up at the top right-hand corner. They were staring at me with a fishy layer over them. His jaw slacks to the side.

'Ma!' I scream.

I don't remember much after that.

2

I open my eyes and it takes a beat to remember where I am. Jaysus, this sofa is not comfortable at all. Makes me wish Ma hadn't converted my room upstairs into a sewing office or some shite. The other bedroom is packed to the gills with crap she won't throw out. Couldn't find a bed in that room if you tried. I take a second to reflect on my mother's hoarding issues and how the generation that grew up with nothing kept everything. When it's her turn to pass, her sons will have to dump all of that shite. What a waste.

'You're awake,' says a voice from the end of the sofa.

I leap up; the twenty-year-old blanket cascades into the air and lands at my feet.

It's Paul. Creepy, Paul.

'What the fuck!' I bark.

'Oowwwwh. Someone is a tad jumpy,' he says in a put-on Welsh accent.

'Why are you being all Jeffery Dahmer on me?'

'Fuckin' hell,' he says, offended. 'I came for breakfast.'

'Where were you last night?' I ask, pulling my jeans on.

–'Double shift.'

'They didn't let you go to your Da's deathbed?'

Paul opens the curtains. Christ, it's bright out. Why is this country so bright? Where is the famous rain when you need it?

– 'To be honest, I didn't even ask.'

'You didn't ask?'

– 'I need the money, you know.'

There it is. He has that hook baited up and is waiting for me to bite.

'You couldn't be that fucking desperate for money,' I say.

–'I am, listen--'

Ma opens the door– a lifesaver.

'Would you be leaving your brother alone and let him sleep,' she commands.

'He's awake,' Paul says.

'D'ya want a fry?' she asks.

I say yes even though I don't want one. But the thought of Paul begging me for money is turning my stomach.

***

I saunter into the kitchen and see a bottle of whiskey on the table. I can feel Kevin's eyes boring into me. He's at the stove, fixated on me and the bottle. I eyeball the bottle and then him. I can tell what's running around his little hamster wheel brain. But this time, it isn't me. I didn't drink last night after the hospital. He returns to the pan full of Superquinn sausages, ensuring they are evenly brown but not black.

Out of nowhere, Ma pulls four glasses from the decades-old cabinet and plonks them on the table. She opens the whiskey and pours generous amounts into each glass.

'C'mere, all of yiz,' she says.

She has the glasses in her hand. I step forward, being the obedient youngest son.

'I have the sausages on,' Kevin says.

'Will yeh put the feckin' pan aside and c'mer,' she growls. Kevin does as he's told. Paul slithers up beside me. We are each handed a glass, and Ma makes less of a toast and more of a battle plan.

'Right,' she yaps, 'today will be hard and tomorrow even harder. I want you three to compose yourselves and be polite to the neighbours and well-wishers. I need someone to come with me to Macy's Funeral Home while David writes the eulogy.'

'I'm not doing the eulogy, Ma,' I can be the stubborn one.

Ma gives me a look.

'Fine,' there's a bass to her tone of voice, 'Kevin, you write the eulogy. David, come with me to the funeral home. Paul, you keep your wife out from under me feet today. I don't need to be fussed upon.'

'Ma?' I say. 'Don't be saying that.'

–'Wha'? I just don't want the fuss, is all.'

'I mean, you could have just said…' I begin.

–'Are we drinking this feckin' whiskey or what?' she explodes. 'It's a tradition on my side of the family that we drink to the dead on the morning after; otherwise, we'll be drinking until it's our turn to be drunk too.'

'I'm not sure that's a saying, Ma,' I say.

- 'I never said it was a saying. I said it was a tradition.' There's anger in her voice. A beast is somewhere inside, dying to get out.

We clink glasses, down the whiskey, and let Kevin return to breakfast.

'Why won't you write the eulogy?' Ma pokes. At this point, I'm at the kitchen table, and she's pacing the floor.

'I told you I don't want to.'

'But you're the writer in this family.'

'Yeah, but I don't want to write his eulogy.'

Things start to heat up in my belly. I hope it's the whiskey.

'Why not?' Ma sounds desperate for an answer.

'Because he was a horrible bastard.'

I feel the air move past my eyebrow. Ma's whiskey glass shatters on the wall behind me before the words finish coming out of my mouth.

'What the–?' is all I can manage.

'I didn't mean that now,' Ma says. It sounds like she woke up from rage and is embarrassed about it. 'I'm– I'm sorry. I– I didn't mean to do that.' Her hands vibrate by her side. 'I'll clean it up.'

'I'll do it, Ma,' Paul says timidly. He already has the broom in hand.

'I'll go get– I'll go get dressed for the funeral home,' she mutters and leaves. She takes the whole atmosphere of the room with her as she disappears up the stairs.

'You had to fucking go and rile her up like that. Can you not just keep your mouth shut,' Kevin mocks from the stove.

–'Oh fuck you, Kevin. She nearly decapitated me with a glass tumbler, and you want to blame the victim.'

'No, fuck you,' Kevin says, pointing a pair of greasy stainless steel prongs at me. 'You came here, Mister Big Shot.'

'You asked me to come, ya prick,' I spat.

I stand to meet Kevin, eye to eye. I can smell his stale breath hidden behind mint chewing gum.

'Every time you come here, you're like a hurricane. But you don't see the disaster when you leave,' he starts.

'What fucking disaster?'

'Why don't you stay at Aunt Catherine's like you always do?' he blurts.

The doorbell saves us. Ma bangs on the floor upstairs. It's a sign to shut the fuck up. But not before I add, 'Go write his fucking eulogy. Make him out to be the big man.'

I wait until I reach the kitchen door before adding a cherry on top of my insult. 'Your sausages are burning.'

– 'Shite!'

***

I open the front door and take a second to remember a face. She's even more surprised to see me.

'David?'

–'Linda.'

'You came back?'

She looks well. Linda Murphy. Jaysus. A name I had not thought about in a long time. She fixes her hair over her ear and looks to the ground for fallen words.

'Kinda had to,' I say.

'I know you didn't, erm, care for him.'

–'I didn't….'

'Listen, I just came to pay my respects.'

–'Do you want to come in?'

Why is she afraid to look at me? Is it because I'm staring at her? She has that strawberry blonde hair that used to be dark red. Then blue, because she was cool like that. Now look at us? Time has taken its toll. We both have a few wrinkles. I've a few grey hairs.

'I can't. I don't think me pram will fit through your hallway.'

That's when I notice the pram. Christ, she has a kid. Why wouldn't she have a kid? She's in her late thirties. I just wasn't expecting it. The last time I saw her was when we were seventeen. Christ, time flies.

'I could, em, watch the… he-she, erm, baby.'

'He,' Linda says. 'He's actually called David, which is awkward now.'

I pinch my lips and try not to laugh at the irony. I love laughing at the irony. Jesus.

'Go on in; I'll mind him. Fucking love talking to fellow Davids."

'You don't mind?'

Irish sayings. You miss them when you live abroad. Like, "you don't mind". It's just us being polite. If I had a problem with it, I wouldn't have asked. I'm not a masochist.

'Ah, no.'

'Thanks,' she says and slips behind me, leaving me with baby David. I look in the pram. There he is. Small, chubby, and asleep. He doesn't look like Linda. She has this square-jawed thing going on, while this kid has a round face. Don't they say that the baby looks like the dad for a while, so he can't deny that it's his? Maybe that's it. Who the fuck does he look like, then?

Ah shite… the baby stirs. I look to the street for help. It's empty. Typical. I scan the pram for a soother.

Nothing.

Shite.

He starts crying. It's pitiful and innocent.

'If I pick you up, will you stop crying?'

I scoop him up from the comfort of the pram and into the crisp morning air.

'What's the craic?' I ask him.

I bounce him up and down, and little David's cries die long enough for him to puke white all over my shoulder. Great.

Aw man, it smells. The cries turn into wails.

'There, there,' I beg.

I'm not exactly the baby whisperer.

'Ah Jesus, look at yeh,' Linda comes to the rescue. She takes her kid, who doesn't look like her, and is about to wipe the puke off my t-shirt with her hand when her brain catches up with actions. Her hand hovers over my shoulder.

'I'm sorry,' she says, looking for a cloth in her baby bag.

'I need to change anyway.'

–'He gets terrible wind.'

'I can tell.'

– 'Jesus, I'm sorry.'

'Don't worry. I have to shower before the funeral home.'

– 'No, I mean about your Da.'

'Ah yeah. Thanks.'

She's about to go for a hug but remembers that I have her offspring's milk on my shoulder.

–'Sorry for your loss,' she says as a parting gift.

'You too.'

–'Wha'?'

'Sorry. I'm new to this.'

Linda laughs and then catches herself. She makes sure no one on the street hears her. I have a little giggle myself.

'Good to see yeh',' I say.

-'You too, David.'

We nod. It's that awkward moment when someone should leave, but we both stand there.

'You look good,' she says.

'You look gorgeous.'

Shouldn't have said that. Stupid asshole. Don't say such things to women who just popped out a kid. Hormones are still on the rampage.

'Erm,' is all she says before jaunting off, baby on her shoulder. She looks back at me as she goes.

Christ, that puke smells.

***

Declan Macy of Macy's Funeral Home was a middle-aged, bald man who wore a long winter jacket indoors even though the heating was cranked up. We were in one of the waiting rooms with thick carpets that made a thump-thump sound when you walked on it. The walls felt close for a large room. The screen mounted on the wall caught my eye. It was a slideshow of one horrible memorial slide after another. *"Rest as you lived." "We honour your life." "You are the immortal memory."*

Declan Macy spoke in a manner that made me question his north-side accent.

'Now, let's write down everything that will appear in the death notice,' he said.

"From Home to Heaven, Godspeed!"

Ma prepared herself by gripping the handles of her oversized handbag. Her knuckles went white as she took a breath.

'So his full name was?'

-'Brian Paul Dowling,' Ma said.

Declan Macy jotted words down on a notepad, reading it aloud as he did. 'Died peacefully at Connolly Hospital surrounded by his loving family. Beloved husband of?'

-'May.'

Loving family?

'Children?' Macy asked.

I'm sitting right here, bud.

'Kevin, Paul, and David,' she said, laying a soft hand on my leg.

'Beloved husband of May and loving father of Kevin, Paul, and David.'

Don't laugh, don't swear.

'Any grandchildren?' He asked.

'No,' Ma said with a hint of venom. She glanced at me: 'Or?'

'Or what?' I said. She just stared at me like I was supposed to have a new answer. 'I don't have any kids.'

Ma nodded.

'Do you think I have hidden kids somewhere?' I tried to whisper, but it was a funeral home. Even the dead could hear me. 'No, it's just –no.' she said dismissively, then added, 'You never know.'

'Did he have any siblings?' Declan changed the subject.

'Just a brother, John.'

Fucking Uncle John. If one person was worse than me Da, it was him.

'Have you got siblings yourself, May?' Declan Macy asked.

'Yes, three sisters and a brother.'

'Any one of yer boys married?'

'Paul is married to a lovely woman, Martina,' Ma proudly said.

Ma hates that woman.

Declan read off his notes rapidly. 'Brian will be sadly missed and remembered with love by his wife May, children Kevin, Paul, and David, daughter-in-law, brother John, sisters-in-law, brother-in-law, nieces, nephews, extended family, neighbours, friends and all who knew and loved him. Family flowers only, donations in lieu of flowers to Connolly Hospital. May He Rest In Peace. Reposing at Declan Macy's Funeral Home this Wednesday between 4 pm and 6 pm. Removal on Thursday to Saint Finian's Oratory, Finglas South, arriving for the 10 am Funeral Mass. Thereafter, to Glasnevin Crematorium.'

Ma reached for the tissue box beside me. I wondered if they were crocodile tears she was shedding. This all seemed like a poorly put-together farce.

'Can you change that,' Ma said suddenly.

'Yes?' Declan Macy cocked an eyebrow.

'I want to have him at home. The old-fashioned way.'

'Wait, what?' I spat.

-'Are you sure, Mrs Dowling?' Macy asked.

'I'm sure.'

'Ma, you can't be serious,' I said, but she didn't look at me. 'Mammy!'

'I've said my piece,' she said sternly.

She said her piece. This is a shit show.

'Now,' Declan Macy says, standing up. 'As for the coffin.'

'Coffin?' I blurted. 'Isn't he getting cremated?'

'Yes, but we need a coffin,' he replied.

'But doesn't he go into a box?'

'A coffin is a box,' me Ma added.

'You know what I mean,' I said and asked Declan, 'How much is a coffin?'

***

He brings us into the coffin room. Fucking hell, you should see the shit people get buried in. There's a Dublin GAA coffin for a true Dubs fan. A wicker coffin for the weirdos.

'I would suggest,' Declan says, 'Since it's a cremation, we should go with the Leinster Wax. It's a veneered oak with a plain-sided finish.'

'Lovely,' Ma says.

'That's what most people get cremated in, is it?' I ask.

'It's the lower range in price,' Declan says.

'I see.'

'Right, we'll go and pick him up from Connolly and get him prepared. Did you bring clothing for him?'

'Yes,' Ma says, taking a plastic bag from her enormous handbag. Now I know she's being defiant. She didn't neatly fold the clothes and place them in a box or a nice leather bag; no, she fucked them in an old Dunnes Stores plastic bag that she must have found in the back of a drawer somewhere. I know my mother, and I know when she's being defiant. But why the viewing at home? Why is she giving him a wake?

'And as for payment?' Declan Macy says behind his desk.

Ma looks at me. I look at her, cocking my eyebrows.

'He had insurance, right?' I say to her.

Ma snaps out of her little trance. Surely, she didn't think I would splash out on a funeral for the bollix.

'That's right, yes,' she says, turning her attention to Declan. 'We need a death certificate for the insurance.'

'I'll put you on credit for now, but we'll have to hold the ashes until everything is paid up,' he says.

'Fair.'

I almost laugh. Holding his ashes for ransom. What would he do with the ashes if we never paid? Piss in them?

'I'll see yeh tomorrow then at about twelve, we'll set up in the living room for yeh,' Declan says and then shakes our hands. 'One last thing. Are you David Dowling, the writer?'

'Yeah.'

'Jaysus. My wife loves your books.'

He lets go of me hand, and we're out of the funeral home. Is the pub open? I need a pint.

'Would you not write the eulogy?' Ma says in the beautiful pity voice she usually reserves for, *"Why won't you find a girl and get married?"* or *"Why can't I have a grandchild?"*

'I wouldn't know what to say Ma.'

I'm being honest. What do you say?

'Make something up then.'

'Ma, I can't just make something up.'

'Don't you literally make up stuff for a living?.'

She had a point.

'I'm gonna be honest with you, it wouldn't be right. Kevin is the oldest. He should do it.'

There's a pause. She cleans the air out of her nose and says, 'You know he'll mess it up.'

'Ahhh, I can't wait,' I say.

3

It's six o'clock. I had an argument with Ma about having the wake at home. She gave valid reasons why she could. The first and most valid one was that it was her house and she could do what she wanted. She had more points but you needn't concern yourself with them. Point number one trumped them all.

I'm trying to hold back the urge to go for a pint until my publisher calls. Apparently, you have to actually provide pages for the advance they give you. She asks me how the book is going. I say it's great. I'm lying through me teeth. I have zero words done. All I have is a bunch of notes that make no sense to anyone other than me. Like this: *Liston (give a good first name, something that punches) is known for two things in this town. 1) being married to a supermodel (give a good supermodel name, Kirstin Badger or something) and 2) for fucking a horse in secondary school. Then he meets Jesus, who will rid the world of all knowledge that he fucked the horse but he has to help him on a covert operation into hell in an attempt to assassinate Lucifer.*

So I tell my publisher everything is great, and I hang up. I tell Ma I need to go somewhere quiet to write.

'Sure, it's quiet here,' Ma says.

She has a point. But just like magic, Kevin can be heard pounding the kitchen table and swearing like there is no tomorrow.

'Ah-yeh-know,' I say, pointing at the wall. I grab me coat and say, 'I'll take a key.'

***

I'm in the village and pop into the Shamrock Inn. I wonder how long this place has been here as I find a spot at the corner of the bar. It's right beside the carvery lunch display, which is empty at this time of the evening. I can hear the cleaners in the kitchen still bashing and clashing pots and pans.

I order a Guinness and flick through some more of my notes on my iPhone.

Man finds out that he is the reincarnation of John Lennon but can't sing.

I delete that one.

An IT startup intercepts alien transmission and tries to sell it to the highest bidder. Bidder is an outcast from the alien race and the richest person on Earth.

Fuck's sake. I delete that, too.

I dunk my top lip in the Gunness and suck the dark heavenly liquid. I run a hand across my lip and read more notes, but the bar's sounds distract me. As I look up, taking in the atmosphere, I spot a middle-aged man staring at me. He's wearing glasses and a shirt covered by a checked jumper. I'm betting he's a banker or a teacher.

'Can I ask you something?' he half-shouts across the bar.

–'Technically you just did.'

I need to stop doing that.

'Technically,' he says. 'Are you David Dowling?'

–'Yep.'

'The writer?'

–'The writer.'

I hate this part.

'Jaysus.'

Why do people keep saying that?

'You saved my life,' this stranger says.

What?

–'Excuse me?' I say.

'Hear me out. I work up at New Cross College-'

–'I don't know what that is.'

'It's the school where all of Patrician College went when it closed down.'

–'It closed down? Shit… I went there.'

'We know. So a kid was reading your latest book in class. The one about the zombies at a hotel resort. So I took it from him.'

–'Kids read?'

'He's a good kid. Too smart for this place. Anyway, so it's a Friday and I'm leaving work about to jump in my car when this kid comes running up saying can he get his book back. I tell him to get it on Monday but then I see the look on this kid's face. Who am I to deny a child from reading?'

–'Especially my book.'

'So I get out of me car and go and retrieve the book. When I come back, me car's on fire.'

–'Fuck off.'

'You're not gonna believe this. It was hit by a meteor.'

–'Fuck off.'

'Look it up.'

–'What do I put in?' The phone is back in my hand.

'New Cross College meteor attack.'

–'Meteor attack,' I say for dramatic effect.

Sure enough, there it is. The article has a picture attached, and the guy sitting next to me is in the picture, standing beside a burned-out Ford Fiesta.

–'Nice jacket,' I say. It's always good to give a compliment. I learned that from my ex.

'I still have it.'

–'Well fuck me, a meteor hit your shitty car.'

'And if it wasn't for you I'd be dead.'

–'Bit of a stretch there, but I'll take it.'

'Next drink is on me,' the teacher says.

-'I'll take that too.' Always accept a drink when offered. I think that saying was passed down from the Boomers to the X-Y-Z generation.

I take the free Gunness and raise a glass.

'What are you in town for? Don't you live in Berlin or something.'

–'Budapest.'

'Lovely place.'

–'It's fucking mental.'

'So why are you back? If you don't mind me asking.'

–'Erm… yeah, me Da just died.'

'Brian is dead?' the barman says, wiping a wine glass. He blesses himself and returns the glass to its hanger.

'You knew me Da?' I ask.

'Jaysus, everyone knows your Da.'

'Ah-yea?'

I didn't know him.

'Great man. When did he go?' the barman asks.

'Last night. Wake is tomorrow at the house. The funeral is on Thursday.'

I don't know why this is making me sad. Water's trying to make its way from the back of me nose to the corners of me eyes.

'I'll be there,' he says. 'Listen,' he adds quietly, 'Next pint is on me.'

I'll take that too. Turning out to be a cheap night.

***

I'm four pints in when I spot Linda Murphy. She comes up to the bar to order. I pretend not to see her. I don't know why.

'Twice in one day,' she says.

I look up and act surprised. 'Howayeh.'

'How's your Ma?'

Jesus, she's gorgeous.

Is that the drink talking?

I only had four.

'She's… well I don't know, to be honest, Ma's never one for open conversation.'

'All mothers are the same,' Linda says.

'Aunty Catherine wasn't like that. She was very vocal.'

'Ah yea'?' Linda's eyes glaze over. The mention of my Aunt Catherine would do that. To Linda, Catherine was the beginning of the end of our relationship.

'How come you're out on a Tuesday?' I say changing the subject.

'Ah it's Friday somewhere.'

No, it's not. Why did she have to ruin it by saying something like that?

'My mom is looking after the little fella, so I'm out for a quick one with a few of the crew,' Linda says and gestures to the corner table close to the exit. There are about five of them, but I'm not really counting. 'Why don't you come over.'

'Ah no.'

'C'mon. It's not every day that your ex-ex-ex boyfriend is a famous writer.'

Ex-ex-ex? Fuck me, I just went off her.

'I won't take no for an answer,' she says.

***

I sit at the edge of the group, or *crew* as Linda calls them. I'm surprised she didn't call them her squad. Fucking buzz words nowadays. She must have had some pre-drinks because she sounds different than this morning.

'C'mer, tell me, David, do you have a big house in Budapest?' one of her crew members asks me. The way she said Budapest: *Buddha-best*.

'No. Small flat.'

'I thought you were fucking famous. Here Linda, I thought you said he was famous.'

'He is,' she says and sips on her Coors Light.

'Small flat, he said.' The common one giggles. 'Couldn't be that fucking famous.'

They all laugh. What am I doing here? Where is that teacher? He can save my life in return. School night. I bet he's gone.

'Got a huge house yerself, love?' I ask.

'Fucking council house,' she squawks. 'Better than a small fucking flat.'

The sheep's laughter follows.

'So what are yeh famous for anyway?' another of the crew asks. I'll call her Tattoo Bitch because I can't remember all their names. She has this massive thing on her neck that could be a spider web. It could be something completely different.

'I'm a writer.'

'Movies?' the *Buddha-best* one says. I'll call her Council House Bitch.

'Novels.'

'Sure, nobody reads anymore,' the Tattooed Bitch says.

'Probably why I have a small flat,' I say.

More laughter. At least I got there first. I look at Linda. She's embarrassed.

'Where yiz somewhere before this?' I ask.

'Just at Linda's doing a bit of pre,' Tattoo Bitch says. Pre-drinking is something that I used to participate in, and now I think it's childish. In case you're unfamiliar with it, dear diary in my head, it is when you go get booze from a shop or off-licence before you go out. You load up on drinks and finish off the night in the pub.

'Bit of coke too,' Council House Bitch adds.

I look at Linda again. She's gone red in the cheeks. Her baby looks brand new. Which means she's breastfeeding. Maybe she's not. Let's hope she's not. None of my business anyway.

'Mad for the coke, aren't ya Linda?' Council House Bitch says.

Why the fuck am I here?

'Jesus Christ, Bernie,' Linda says in a hushed tone, 'His Da just died, and you're ripping the piss out of him.'

I stand, 'Ah no, don't let the death of my Da stop yeh from being bitches. Carry on.'

I make my way to the door. As I do, I hear, 'Who the fuck do you think you are,' and 'Fucking hotshot calling us bitches.'

'Yeah, might be bitchin', but you're not a bitch,' I hear Tattoo Bitch say. I'm gonna remember that line.

Outside, the air stings the nose. The evenings now are for jacket wearers, and I left mine at home. I suddenly crave a cigarette, a double burger and chips with lots of salt and vinegar. Jesus, I haven't thought about smoking in years. That prick's death is bringing out the worst in me. I head towards the Mace Newsagents on the corner of Main Street. They sell everything there. Except for burgers and chips, that is.

'David?' I hear Linda say.

I turn to see that she, too, has forgotten her jacket.

'Listen,' she says, 'I'm sorry.'

'Sorry,' I say. The word drifts off into infinity. 'Everyone is sorry, Linda, but they don't know for what.'

'I'm sorry about your Da,' she tries to add comfort to her intonation.

'But are yeh?'

She doesn't know what to say.

'Can I get your number.' she says, looking for her next words on the pavement. 'You know, in case we want to meet up while you're here. Talk about the good old times.'

I try to smile and dig my hand into my jeans. I hand her a card from my wallet and say goodnight.

***

I have a buzz on me now, but I don't want to try another bar. Not now. The "crew" ruined it for me. I pass the off-licence and decide to pop in for a take-out.

I navigate to the cold beers and grab a six-pack. Christ it's expensive. How does the run of the mill, working class person afford to have a drink at the weekend? Poxy government.

'Are sure there he is…' a voice says behind me.

I turn to see the cashier behind the counter with a big thick smile on his face.

'Ah Jaysus,' I say.

I don't recognise him but he recognises me. Now, I've been in this situation before where I can't remember that I've met someone and then have a follow-up conversation about the conversation I can't remember. Smiley here looks like he knows me. So I'll play along for the moment. It has also happened that sometimes people just act like they know you because they have seen you on some chat show promoting a book that no one reads, apparently.

'How's it going?' I ask.

'Ah grand,' Smiley says. He scans the beer and adds. 'You've put on the weight, haven't yeh? Is this it, is it?'

He's holding up the beer like it's Simba from The Lion King. Cheeky bastard. Who the fuck does he think he is?

'Ah, I'm only messin' with yeh,' he says with a chuckle.

'I'm sure you are.'

I hand him cash and wait for me change. He does look familiar. He has that look like he used to be skinny but then found out that his thirties were an express train to Fatville because he didn't look after himself. I'm trying to add hair to him and less cheeks. The teeth! The teeth look familiar. The crooked canines and that little gap in the middle teeth.

'Remember Mrs O'Houlihan? You used to call her Mrs Hooligan,' he says with another chuckle.

Fuck! I know him from school.

'Yeah, that's where the name comes from. Hooligan comes from the name O'Houlihan.'

'Yeah, yeah, yeah,' he blurts. I know he doesn't know that, by the way he's acting. He's trying to play it cool.

Christ I could have been him. If I had stayed in the house and lived in Finglas I could have been… Pádraig? No, that's not his name. James? No.

'There you are, Anto!' A customer says as he enters the shop.

Anto!

Anto, short for Anthony. That's his name.

'Are you working here long, Anto?' I ask him.

'Yeah, got kicked off the building sites, you know? Too much of the party powder, you know?'

'Yeah?'

No, I don't know.

'Yerself? Still writing?' he asks while handing me back the change.

'Still writing.'

That's a lie. I haven't written anything in ages. He doesn't know that.

'Anything else?' Anto asks.

'You wouldn't have smokes would yeh?'

***

I drink three fast beers on the walk home.

I use the key to get in, but I'm drunk. It takes forever, but I eventually make it through the door.

It's eerily quiet. Kevin must have gone home because all the lights are off. I make it to the kitchen, barely.

On the table are three folded A4 pages. I crack a new can and have a little nosy at the pages. Is this the eulogy that Kevin was cursing over earlier? I'm trying to stop me eyes from closing and start reading.

'Fathers, like mothers, are pillars in the development of a child's emotional well-being. They lay down the rules and enforce them. And we look to our fathers to provide a feeling of security, both physical and emotional.'

I see red.

I crack open a can and get to work.

4

The next thing I remember is dreaming I was hurtling towards Earth from space. I was spinning from the black void to the big blue ball. Rinse and repeat. And just as I was about to burn up in the atmosphere, I woke up.

I wish I hadn't.

'Yeh couldn't leave it, could yeh?' Kevin says.

He's looming over me like some Greek ogre. I'm trying to figure out what I did wrong.

'What?'

That's when he wallops me right in the gut.

'What the fuck?' I shout. I'm barely awake at this stage.

***

Turns out I "corrected" Kevin's eulogy. I don't have a 100% recollection of doing this, but it sounds like something I would do. He would say I rewrote it over his initial handwriting, much like a teacher would correct a dyslexic kid's essay.

So instead of saying: *'Fathers, like mothers, are pillars in the development of a child's emotional well-being. They lay down the rules and enforce them. And we look to our fathers to provide a feeling of security, both physical and emotional.'*

It now says: '*Fathers, like mothers, are pillars in the development of a child's emotional well-being.* **Or so they say.** **They** should *lay down the rules and enforce them* **in a safe manner, instead of beating the shit out of them using a telephone book so the neighbours can't see the bruises**. *And we look to our fathers to provide a feeling of security, both physical and emotional.* **Not my father. He was a tyrant who secretly read Mein Kampf.**'

Yeah…

So I'm sitting in the kitchen with a sore belly and a throbbing headache. Ma walks in and looks at me.

'Weeping Jesus on the cross, what happened to you?'

'Your son punched me in the stomach' I say. I always loved ratting him out to Ma.

'That's why you look like that?' she says.

Kevin is making breakfast again. Does he just come around to make breakfast? I know he lives across the street, but Jaysus Ma can make her own breakfast. I've seen her do it many times in the seventeen years I've lived here.

'He's a cunt,' Kevin says, not even looking up from the pan.

The smell of sausages cooking is turning me stomach.

'Don't use the C-U-Next-Tuesday word in my house,' Ma says.

There she goes again with the "my house" thing. She's making a claim on her territory. The alpha male is gone, and now the luna wolf is in charge. She's laying down the law… good for her.

'What did you do?' she growls at me.

'I can't… remember,' I say. I actually can't.

'Me bollix,' Kevin says. 'You can't leave it alone, can yeh?' He is facing me now, egg spatula in hand. Grease flicks off the end like an Olympic diver. 'You always have to…' he trails off, unsure what to say. 'You can't just leave me alone, can yeh?'

'Leave you alone to do what?' I say. It's time to get to the bottom of this shite between him and me. 'To do what?' I repeat. 'Work your nine-to-five, go to the gym and watch Netflix? What the fuck are you doing in life? Besides trying to control mine whenever I'm around.'

'Whenever you're around? People have to die for you to visit.'

Was that an attempt at a comeback?

I shake me head. 'You're fucking terrible with words.'

'Enough!' Ma bellows. 'That's enough. Now I need to clean this house before Mr Macy gets here. I need you-,' she points at me with a wiry finger, '-to go to the shops and get drinks and snacks for later. I'm sure you can handle that; you love the feckin' drink.'

Kevin sniggers.

'And you,' that twig-like finger pointing at Kevin now. 'Finish that breakfast and help me move the furniture in the living room. This house needs cleaning.'

Ma's pissed off. We boys know not to move a muscle for the next five seconds unless we want to see violence. We wait for our signal.

'Now,' she barks.

That's the signal. I'm out the kitchen door and up the stairs for a shower.

***

The walk to the shops is nostalgic and sad at the same time. Ma made me use the chequered shopping trolley to take back the drinks and snacks. I look like an idiot, but me back, shoulders, and arms will be grateful for her decision later.

The Dunnes Stores Shopping Centre on Cardiffsbridge Road brings back a flood of memories. There's a low wall that surrounds the mall and a large open car park that could fit a football pitch on it. The wall is uniform grey now, but I think it used to be dark orange. Maybe I'm mistaken. Memories tend to do that.

Jaysus, Paul's Newsagents is still there. I take a peek inside. They still have the high counter with chocolates and bars in front of it. Lotto and smokes behind it. I remember buying 2000AD comics every week— or when we could afford them. There were also those monthly magazines that had a collectible with them. Kevin got the collection of classic books while I collected football figures that looked like the caricatures of players from the premier league. I also remember buying my first ten-pack of cigarettes there. They didn't even ask me for I.D. Those were the days.

In Dunnes, I roam the aisles looking at the price of things. Jesus, who can afford to live on these prices? Okay, they have the two-for-one deals with meat and biscuits, but Christ, how does a family get by?

I load up on beer and wine and one or two spirits. I grab mixers (buy 3 cokes for 5 euros) and nibbles (no deals on them). I stock up on ham and cheddar and grab three loaves of bread for sandwiches. I don't even want to tell you what I spent.

I tetris the shopping into the granny trolley when I notice a small boy staring at me. He has this curious look on his face, almost like he's concentrating on a quiet fart. I stop what I'm doing and stare back at him. Matching his energy.

'You're famous,' he says while his mam transfers their food from the checkout into paper bags.

'Am I?' I say.

'There's a picture of you in my school where all the famous people go.'

'Is there?'

'Yeah, but I don't know what you're famous for.'

'Me neither,' I say.

'Jake,' the boy's mam says. 'Leave that man alone.'

'But Ma, he's famous.'

'Nobody cares,' his mam says.

That's true. I don't even know why they call me famous. I guess in a place like this, if you make a name for yourself, the whole shitein' town wants to cling to that and spread it so that more and more kids concentrate on something other than sex, drugs and the occasional stint in Mountjoy prison. I've become the "be more like".

'Be more like David Dowling and get an education.'

'Be more like David Dowling and do your homework. Do you think he can live somewhere foreign without a proper education? He's rich now, you know.'

I wish I was rich.

I'm surprised I'm not hated more.

***

I drag the shopping home to find Martina, Paul's wife, standing outside the house. She is on her phone.

She's always on her phone.

I consider her for a second. She's changed a bit. She is more heavy-set, spends far too much time doing her make-up, and wears clothes about two sizes too small for her. I suspect she's a bit mentally disabled, but Ma says she's grand. She doesn't cheat on Paul. She makes him dinner when he gets home from work. What more does he want? She does love spending money, though. I heard once, from Ma, that she spent over two grand on Christmas presents one year.

'You alright, Martina?' I say.

'I heard you got punched in the stomach.'

'Word gets around. Why are you standing outside?'

'Your Ma said I was in the way. So I stepped out here.'

'Jesus! Could you have not gone into the kitchen?'

'It's alright. I'm always in the way.'

I love my mother to bits, but sometimes she can be a right cow to Martina.

'Paul really needs to talk to you,' she says just before I go inside. This is code: *"Paul needs another loan on the loan that you've already lent him, which he's neglected to pay back."*

I want to shout in her face, '*Stop spending money like you're Kim Kar-fucking-dashian and pay me back the money I've loaned*'. But I don't. I smile and nod slightly. She smiles back. She thinks I'm going to give him money. She'd be fucked if I'll give him a single Irish cent.

Inside is chaos. Paul is helping Kevin shift heavy furniture while Ma creeps up behind them with the Dyson vacuum cleaner. I hear Paul curse at Kevin for not using his weight. I hear Ma shout at Paul for shouting at Kevin, so I escape into the kitchen. I unload the shopping into the fridge and cupboard. I could do with one of those beers now, but they're warm.

'Stop being a prick,' Paul howls from the living room.

'Would yeh leave the poor fella alone,' distant Ma says to Paul.

The headache is coming back. I need a coffee.

I could write sonnets about coffee. Soliloquies about the amber colour that grips the lip of me cup. I made Ma get the good stuff from the shops before I even arrived in Ireland. I breathe in the sweet aroma and savour the silence in the kitchen before the occasional bump, swear and vacuum.

Me phone buzzes. It buzzes all the time, but on this occasion, I actually pay some sort of attention to it. One new TikTok message. TikTok message? I don't even remember setting up TikTok. I click the notification and read the DM.

My name is Killian. Sorry about your dad. Can I have an interview?

Straight to the point, Killian. I like that. There's too much fluff in correspondents lately. You have to see how the person is doing. Ask about their day, even though you don't give a shit, give a compliment, and then ask your fucking question. Killian here, straight to the point. Can I have an interview?

I write, *Yeah, go on*. I don't know why. I probably shouldn't have. Ah, sure, fuck it. It's one interview.

He writes back immediately. When I say immediately, he must have been looking at his phone when I wrote.

Great! I'm outside your door.

Fucking creep.

I head for the front door, 'Ma? Where do you keep the hurley stick?'

'Under the stairs,' she says from the living room. This is a question that usually involves a follow-up question of "Why do you need it?" But not for me, Ma.

I collect the Hurley stick from under the stairs and place it behind the door. For those of you wondering what a Hurley stick is, first off, thanks for buying my book. Secondly, it's a stick with a wide, flat, oval end, used in the game of hurling.

So I open the door to a teenager. He has that stupid haircut every teenager in Dublin has and is wearing a dark blue tracksuit, like every other stupid eejit in Dublin.

'Thanks very much, David. This is an honour,' the kid says. He's holding a brand-new iPhone. I don't even have a brand-new iPhone.

I feel bad about getting the Hurley stick now. Maybe. We'll see what stupid questions he has first.

'Can we do the interview now?' he asks.

–'What's this for, school?'

'No, TikTok.'

–'What?'

'It's a TikTok interview.'

–'Should you not be in school?' My voice must have gone up a notch because he cocks his upper lip at me. Martina looks at us like we're dickheads. She buries her head back into her own phone.

'Ready?' The kid says and raises his phone.

–'For what?'

'I'm here with David Dowling. Best-selling author and Finglas-born time traveller.'

Sweet suffering Jaysus!

'Tell me, David,' he says and spins the camera to me. I'm scolding. 'How do you do it? How do you travel through time?'

–'Are you taking the piss? It's me Da's wake today, and you're making fun of me?'

I'm milking this funeral thing within an inch of its life. Pun intended.

He lowers the phone, baffled.

'Do you not know?' he asks.

–'Know what?'

'You're trending.'

–'Wha'? Good trending or bad trending?'

'What's that mean?'

–'I mean, am I Harvey-fucking-Weinstein trending or trending like, you know, whatever cool people think is cool.'

'Ah, no. You're cool,' he says, then adds, 'Who's Harvey Weinstein?'

'Jesus…'

'C'mer and I'll show yeh,' he says, standing closer to me. He holds up his screen and shows me some TikTok videos.

It's a typical TikTok setup. Some American college brat is speaking into the camera.

'You're not gonna believe who's a time traveller?' the college brat says. A legend above his head reads "Famous Time Travelers, Part 3".

The camera cuts to old video footage from the nineties. I recognise the green, single-decker buses on O'Connell Street.

'Bestselling author David Dowling from Dublin was born in 1985 but is shown in this footage in 1990 as a fully formed adult. Watch.'

The camera cuts to an RTE interview outside of the Four Courts post office. A woman is talking, but we can't hear her. In the background, you can see me walking by.

'Jaysus, he does look like me,' I say.

The camera cuts to a late-night interview of me (the actual me) on some promotional tour. Judging by me clothes, I'd say it's the "Greenroom" book promotion.

'As you can see, it's clearly the same person,' the voice-over says.

I've seen enough.

'Jaysus! And people believe this?' I ask the kid.

'Ah yeah, there's loads of them. There's one like, of JayZ at the Taoiseach's wedding, but before he was the Taoiseach. When he was younger and like, eh, a TD or something. He's in the background.'

-'That's mad, huh?'

'Yeah, there's one like with, erm, what's his name… John Wick-'

-'Keanu Reeves-'

'That's him.'

-'Yeh, but he's immortal, not a time traveller.'

'Can we do a TikTok now?' he asks.

-'Hurry before the limo gets here.'

'You're Da's coming in a limo?'

-'They do it for funerals, yeah.'

'I wouldn't know, I've never been to one.'

-'Not yet… C'mon.'

The kid raises his phone again. 'I'm here with David Dowling. Best-selling author and Finglas-born time traveller. Tell me, David, how do you do it? How do you time travel?"

I place my finger to my temple and say, 'With me mind. Use books to travel anywhere, any time and any place.'

Get the point across, David. Buy books. Buy my books.

The kid's not buying it. He drops the phone to his side.

'That's all yeh got?' he says with a bit of a lip.

The little prick.

'The fuck do yeh want? I'm not a time traveller, yeh gobshite. Go to school. Get an education and the fuck out of me garden.'

I may be over-reacting.

The kid switches gears from friendly to pure cunt in two-point-three seconds.

'I probably earn more money than you, yeh bollix. Go suck me dick.'

'That's yer response? You want me to have sexual relations with yeh? It's a bit weird. I'm not gay, though. Or curious. Or a pedo, so I think you need to pick a better argument next time.'

'Fuck off,' he says as he slams the gate on his way out of the garden. I can see his brain milk churning, thinking of a response. 'Glad yer dad's dead.'

I laugh hard. 'Me too.'

This puts a bit of clarity back into him. 'Fucking nut job,' he mutters as he goes. He flips me the bird as the limousine turns the corner. Do I have to dress up?

5

I spruce myself up in the upstairs bathroom. Not that there's a downstairs bathroom. I throw on a black shirt and jeans, also black. I leave the stubble on my chin, though. It makes me look worn. I need to keep up appearances.

I haven't gone to see the body yet.

Is it a body? Is a body still called a body when there is nothing left inside? Is it not a cadaver or a shell? Shite, I have to look it up. A quick Google search later, and I was wrong: *If the organs were preserved by the pathologist, they might be returned to the body, with the exception of any organs that the pathologist needs to retain for later examination. The organs will be placed in plastic bags before being placed back in the body, which is then sewn closed.* So, it is a body. Huh.

Paul and Martina are standing outside the door of the living room.

'Do we have to dress up?' Paul says. He's in his work jeans and a sweat-soaked t-shirt.

'I think that's what they do on these sorts of occasions,' I say.

Paul pauses for a comical beat before saying, 'Fuck, I have to hurry.'

He goes to leave, but Martina whispers in his ear. They look at me. Paul dismisses her and heads out. Jaysus, they're desperate. What sort of band of misfits was I born into?

That's when I see him. Him. The Da. The now dead Da.

I pause.

His coffin takes up most of the living room. You think you have a big living room until they stick a coffin in it.

Jaysus, he looks plastic. I wonder why the embalming process made him look like a wax figure. I'm still not convinced it's him. He looks so gaunt. Christ, they glued his hands together. You can actually see the glue. That's not very good workmanship, is it?

I'm examining him now like he's a piece of art. I'm looking for the seams and the thread. If they had glued his fucking hands properly, I wouldn't be doing this.

'You need to touch the body,' Ma says. She's placing flowers into vases around the fireplace. A fireplace that used to be real, then they got rid of it in favour of central heating. Now she has a fake one put in.

'Wha'?' I say.

'You need to touch the body,' she repeats.

Is she taking the piss? My Ma has an odd sense of humour. She likes those Carry On movies. Tell you one thing: the #metoo movement would not have let those movies pass nowadays.

'Why do I need to touch the body, Ma?'

'If you don't touch the body, he'll come back and haunt yeh.'

'Seriously?'

'If you don't believe in it, you don't have to. I don't have to live with yeh,' she says as she stands beside me Da, caressing his hand.

Declan Macy is at the living room door. Ma goes, leaving me with the body.

I'm going to do it.

I reach out sheepishly and place a hand on his poorly glued hands.

Jaysus, he's freezing.

I look up. Kevin is in the doorway. He's smiling at me. Are they taking the piss out of me? People are starting to come to pay their respects.

***

'Too much for yeh, son?'

Declan Macy is standing in front of me. I'm in the backyard smoking. He pulls out a smoke and lights up.

'Do you mind?' he asks.

'Free country since the twenties,' I say with a smirk.

He chuckles.

'Tell me something,' I say, killing the silence between us. 'Is it hard work?'

'Being a funeral director? I'd say it is.'

'Do you not know?'

'I dunno,' he says. 'Work is work. I mean I think what you do is impossible that's why I don't write. Well, except for the death notices. I do them.'

-'Fair play.'

'So I don't actually know if it's hard work. I've been doing it since I was a teenager, like.'

'Yeah, but does it not take a toll on yeh, seeing grief day in and day out?'

'Ah yeh,' he says, taking a drag for dramatic effect. 'I used to drink… Jesus!… Took some pills. This was years ago. Back when me heart and liver could take it. Almost ran myself into the grave. But then,' he smirks at me. 'Then I realised what they do in the funeral home….'

He leaves the story there, hanging in the Finglas air.

'Wait, what do they do?'

We both chuckle and stub out our cigarettes. I can feel the mood shift as he turns to me.

'I see one of the worst days in people's lives every working day of my life. But you know what? Death is not the end.'

Ah, here we go.

'Whether it's heaven or hell or whatever people want to believe, that's not my place to judge, but the night before a funeral is when you see shit.'

What?

'What?' I say.

'You'll see tonight. The soul or whatever you want to call it. It rebels.'

My eyebrows arch like a Venice bridge, 'What?'

He leaves me with that.

If anyone should know about hauntings, I'm sure it's him.

***

'I'm sorry for your troubles.'

There are those words again. I smile, thank them, shake their hands and move on to the next person. I don't even know half the people here. I scan the room for a family member or even a familiar face. I spot one.

Linda Murphy is at the living room door with the baby in hand. She's looking for someone. I bet it's me. I walk past the crowd of 'sorry for your troubles' and say 'Hi.'

'Ah, there yeh are David. Sorry for–' she starts.

–'My troubles?'

'No, my friends. They were dicks.'

'Your friends need dicks. Lots of them.' I smile.

She has a giggle. 'Jesus, David. Don't make me laugh at a funeral.'

'Technically, this is a wake.'

'Technically,' she mocks me. Her head doing that bobblehead shake.

I look at the kid. He reminds me of someone. Christ, who could it be?

'How's the baba?' I ask, already forgetting his name.

'Baby David is doing fine. Terrible colic though.'

David! How did I forget that!

'There he is! Man of the hour!' a voice bellows from the hall.

I turn. It takes a second to register the face. He's a lot older now and heavier.

'Paddy Cullen?' I say.

He lets out a loud 'Ahhh,' and then tries to mock punch me in the stomach. I don't move. Don't play along.

'What's the story?' Paddy roars. His indoor voice is shite. His funeral viewing voice is even worse.

'Ah, yeh know,' I say. 'Dead Da.'

'Oh, yeh. Sorry for your troubles. I know you hated him.'

'Paddy,' Linda barks.

'What?' he says. 'You told me he hated his Da.'

I can feel everyone's eyes boring into the back of me head. This prick is so loud.

'In confidence,' Linda says and hands Paddy the baby.

Ah, shit. That's why the baby's face looks familiar. It's fucking Paddy Cullen's kid. The bastard who used to beat the shit out of me in school. He picked on me because he was a dumb cunt who probably has undiagnosed dyslexia or some other disorder that hindered his education, so he wanted to restrict mine. Total, epic prick.

'Sorry about this,' Linda says.

'If you spend your time saying sorry for the people you hang around with, it says more about you than it does about them,' I say and move past Paddy without excusing myself.

'Was that a fucking dig at me?' Paddy says to no one.

***

I think I'm getting a fever. The little gust of wind stings as it crosses me face. I try to catch me breath in the front garden. I'm sweating like a priest in an orphanage. I try to control myself, but all I'm getting is sense memory flashbacks.

I'm in secondary school trying to take down me homework for that day. It's an English class, and I'm in the third year. Junior Cert year. Ma says it's important to pass all the exams because if you don't pass your junior, then you're fucked for the rest of your life. Nothing like a bit of pressure for a fifteen-year-old.

I'm almost finished taking the notes down when a hand lands on my exercise book. It's Paddy-fucking-Cullen. He scrunches up my notes and fucks it across the room just in time for the end of lesson bell.

'That's what you get, swot,' he says and then spits on my copybook.

I stay an extra few minutes and frantically write down the homework. Mrs Green, the English teacher, is not happy. I am taking up her break, but I think she is more unhappy with me for not standing up for myself. She even gives me a cryptic clue.

'Do you ever notice that the people who hate themselves seem to want others to hate themselves too? The infliction of suffering soothes them,' Mrs Green says, not even looking up from her newspaper.

'Who said that, Miss?' I say, thinking it's a quote.

She looks me dead in the eye. 'I did. Just now. Can you please get out of my classroom, Mister Dowling?'

When I get outside, my whole class is sniggering at me. I get catcalls and hear slurs of 'Are yeh riding the teacher now, David?' and 'Teacher's pet'. Paddy Cullen rushes up to me and punches me hard in the stomach. I can't catch my breath.

'You better not have ratted me out,' he says through his teeth.

The rest of the class laughs at this.

I fucking hated school.

And I fucking hated Paddy Cullen.

See, he got into trouble about something unrelated during the day. He thought I ratted him out, and he took it up with me on the trek home from Patrician College. He made sure I never got hit in the face. But the body shots were hard. They hurt for a long time after that beating. I could feel the anger in him with every hit to the ribs and stomach. I could see him retract in pain as his knuckles connected with bone. That made him more angry.

Standing in me Ma's garden now, I think about who he was angry at. It wasn't me. I was his punching bag, his release. I wonder if he had a Da like mine. If I had it bad, he must have had it worse.

Or…he could just be a cruel cunt. There are plenty of them in the world without having to have an excuse to hide behind.

Speaking of cruel cunts. I see one parking his car now. Uncle-Fucking-John.

I make a note of the make and brand of the car and come up with a cunning plan to piss him off before disappearing back inside. It is time for a drink, or seven.

***

I sit down in the kitchen beside Paul and Kevin. I hand them each a beer. Kevin pushes the can away without saying anything. When Uncle John walks in, he changes his mind. He cracks the can and takes a huge gulp.

Uncle John, the cruel cunt. He's the image of me Da. Well, not now, but when me Da was bulky and strong. This fucker has a horse's neck, buzz cut and a walk that says, *"look at me, hard as nails."* The prick is in his sixties and is probably fitter than I am.

'There he is,' he announces to the kitchen, 'Mister Famous.'

His inner-city drawl is like a thousand pins pricking me eardrums.

'John,' I say.

He takes a stool on the other side of the table. He makes it look like a child's stool, the size of the bollix.

'Too famous to give your own uncle a hug?'

I smile at him. He's not getting to me. I notice that Paul and Kevin have their heads in their cans of beer. Martina, parked beside Paul, has hers in a brand-new Samsung phone that I probably bought for her.

'Mister Educated has come back to pay his respects. Can't call his Da when he is alive, but can drink his beer at his wake. Who paid for that education?'

I have a feeling he's gonna fuck this argument up. Can't wait.

'That's right, your Da,' he says.

Wrong! Ya dickhead! I paid for it with me own money. The money I earned by selling a screenplay for a little independent movie that got picked up at the Sundance Film Festival. I was given points for the film so I received a percentage of the film's net proceeds (each point is 1%). I paid for me own fucking college. I won't say that, though. Out of respect for me Ma, I won't have an argument in the kitchen the day of her husband's wake.

'You doing well for yerself, John?' I ask. Hopefully, this will give him what he needs…a soapbox to talk about himself.

'Ah yeah. I parked me beamer outside. D'you see it? I know you saw it. D'you have a beamer?' he asks.

The way he says "Do you" or "D'you" sounds like "Jew". This gives me inspiration to take the piss out of this ape of a man.

'No, I don't have a BMW. That's a Nazi car, isn't it?' I say.

-'Piss off,' he says, not sure if I'm messing.

'It's true. My education told me so. They built engines for the Nazi regime using slave labour from concentration camps. Same with that Hugo Boss jacket you're wearing there. They made SS uniforms. Next you'll be telling me you own a pair of Adidas.'

Martina looks at me and then tries to hide her black Adidas runners under her chair.

'I'm no fucking Nazi,' he threatens.

'I'm not saying that. I'm saying that you're driving and wearing something that is associated with the Nationalsozialistische Deutsche Arbeiterpartei at a particular time in history. There's Jewish blood on that cloth and in your engine.'

'Are you being smart?'

'You fucking told me I was smart, didn't yeah?' I snarl at him. 'You called me Mister Educated, so I'm fucking educating yeh.'

I don't know why I said that. That was a stupid idea. I just started a fucking argument when I said I wouldn't.

I'm an ant picking a fight with an elephant.

It's dead silent. I can see Kevin anticipating a swinging fist with my name on it. Paul is cringing.

I think Uncle John is about to burst a vein in his horse's neck.

Then he laughs. A hearty laugh.

'You got me,' he says between barrels of laughter.

I take a breath. I see Kevin's shoulders relax. I think Paul is about to faint. Martina laughs at something on her phone.

I stand. 'I'll get yeh a beer,' one last dig incoming, 'The ones that I bought. Not only am I famous, I'm rich too.'

I laugh. Fake.

He laughs. I think it's fake.

'My man,' he said.

I am not your fucking man.

John drinks his Heineken in two gulps.

'Can't beat a Heinie, can yeah?' he says.

He shakes the empty bottle at me. The Dowling boys are dead still at the table. Uncle John looks at his empty bottle and then at me. It's that slow look that my Da used to do before he unleashed hell.

I get the shivers.

The shivers ignite a flame in my stomach.

'Are you miming for another beer?' I say, my voice going up slightly. 'Use your fucking words.'

I stand to approach the fridge.

'Excuse me?' he says. He wasn't begging for pardon. There was a threat in that question.

It is extremely silent. I hear the scrape of wooden legs on a tiled floor. I'm expecting a sucker punch as I open the fridge door.

'He said, use your fucking words.' I turn to see Kevin standing.

John crooks his trunk neck. Is Kevin standing up for me? Literally and figuratively? I'm in awe.

A small shape enters the kitchen.

'D'ya not want to see your brother?' Ma has a hand that lands on John's shoulder.

He turns to see his sister-in-law. 'Jayus, May. Sorry for your troubles.'

He's not sorry for ours, though. Prick.

'He's in there. We'll get the sandwiches.'

John nods. He rises and disappears into the living room. We hear him wailing like a banshee a few moments later.

'I'll make the sandwiches, Ma,' Kevin says.

'No, Martina will.'

Martina looks up. 'Yeah,' she says. She doesn't know what she's saying yes to.

***

John and most of the mourners leave after an hour. I had a fill of Martina-made sandwiches, and I've had about four drinks now. Kevin is up there with me. Round for round. Which is surprising because I had never seen him drink before. Except when me Ma forced a whiskey into him the other day. Paul is quiet, as usual. Ma finally comes to sit down and have a drink. I pour her a whiskey cola.

'More cola than whiskey there, son.'

'He's a fucking madman,' Kevin says to Ma. He's nodding his chin at me.

'Why is he a mad man?' Ma asks unbeknownst.

'He called Uncle John a Nazi and got away with it,' Paul burst in.

'You called John a Nazi?' Ma asks.

'Not me proudest moment,' I say.

Ma bursts out laughing. She's red in the face. 'Jesus, fair play,' she bellows and gives me a huge kiss on the cheek.

'I love my sons,' she continues, grabbing Paul and Kevin's hands. She rests her head on my shoulder.

I want to cry. It's going to come at some stage– the tears.

'Can I ask you something?' I say. I want to ask a hundred questions, but I only want to know this one right now. I look through the kitchen doors to the living room. The last of the mourners, Mr Jones from down the street, leaves. He gives a little wave on his way out. The house is finally quiet now.

'Go on,' she says.

'Are you relieved?' I ask.

This floors her. I can see it in her eyes. Her lower lid starts to glisten.

'I love my sons.' She squeezes her son's hands and downs her drink. 'I'd love another drink.'

'Me too,' Martina says.

Just then, the three mad aunts walk in. Me ma's sisters. God must have hated my Granny because he gave her three sonic booms with dust on them and me Ma and uncle Pat, for good measure.

'Time to get our drink on,' Aunty Grace says. She's the skinny one with leathery skin from too many trips to Santa Ponsa. She has that bleached blonde hair and blue eyeshadow, for some reason. None of them even look at me Da. They beeline straight to me Ma.

'That taxi fella was gorgeous, wasn't he?' Aunty Cora says. She's the youngest at 62 and the loudest. She was the first in line to get one when divorce was passed in Ireland.

'Jesus, Cora, act your feckin' age,' Aunty Catherine says. She's the strict one. My second mammy. She is short like me Ma, but kept her school teacher manner even after retiring from the job six years ago. Got some mouth on her, though. She spots me getting up to take a piss.

'Your last book was not good,' she tells me.

'Says you and the Turkish government,' I tell her.

'The Turkish government?' Ma asks.

'I'll tell yeh when I get back.'

***

Paul finally got his chance to talk to me outside the bathroom. He stumbles over his words like a banjaxed horse in a hurdles race.

'It's just,' Paul strutters. 'I need, erm— I need to talk.'

–'Um-hm?'

'Remember that loan I took off yeh?'

–'How can I forget? That loan was my new kitchen. My kitchen is islandless. I want an island in me kitchen.'

'Why would you put an island in your kitchen?'

'A kitchen island, yeh gobshite. You know, the oven is behind yeh, the island is in front of yeh, you can cook and chop shit while looking at yer guests.'

'Oh…'

'Oh, anyway, go on,' I say, 'You have my attention.'

'I have your money,' Paul says. 'All of it.'

I'm confused. 'Ah, my island awaits.'

'I'm not, eh, I'm… fuck it. I'll transfer the money later.'

Paul storms downstairs and out the door. Martina flies after him. She mutters 'prick' on the way out.

I try to decipher what just happened.

***

'Why does Turkey not like you?' Ma asks after the fifth drink.

We're all a bit giddy.

'Because I'm not a vegan?'

I must be drunk. That joke didn't land.

'That was a bad joke.' At least Ma agrees with me.

'Have you not read me last book?' I ask her.

'Your books always start so well and then they go all weird,' says Ma.

Aunty Catherine nods her head in agreement.

'Well the last book is set in a Turkish resort full of all-inclusive guests.'

'Why would the government be annoyed about that?' Ma asks.

'Then there's a zombie outbreak and they have to survive for three days until the Turkish army gets there.'

'There you go, see? Weird stuff,' Ma says. 'Why can't you write a romance like that, erm, Ahern one. What's her name? The P.S. I Love You girl. Bertie's daughter.'

'Cecelia.'

'That's her,' Ma says.

'She has good novels,' Aunty Catherine adds.

'Why would I write romantic novels?'

'For the romance,' Ma says.

I stare at my Ma. Romance is something she probably hadn't felt in a long time.

'Anyway. Turns out the Turkish government, or at least, someone in the Turkish embassy of Hungary doesn't like the way I portrayed the Turkish people and their army.'

'Why? What did you write?' Kevin says.

'Does no one read my novels?'

'Nobody reads,' Kevin replies.

'I keep hearing that,' I say, hurt. Not really. I couldn't give a shit. I send me free copies home anyway. 'At the end of the novel, spoiler alert for something you won't fucking read anyway, the Turkish army comes in and only takes the Turkish nationals from the resort, leaving the main characters to fend for themselves.'

'Jesus,' Kevin says.

'There is a petition to have me banned from entering the country.'

'Really?' Ma asks, concerned.

'No, of course not. Nobody gives a shit about the written word any more. It's all vlogs and tweets.'

'So what is the plan for the night?' Aunty Catherine asks, changing the subject.

'What do you mean?' I say.

'One of ye have to stay with the body while your Ma gets some rest,' Aunty Grace adds. She nods to me Ma, who falls asleep on Kevin's shoulder.

'I'll stay,' Kevin says.

'No,' I say. 'Sure, me bed is in there with him anyway.'

'You sure you want to do that?' Aunt Catherine says. 'Your room is always made up at mine.'

I smile. That woman is always there for me. There is a warmth to her that only I can feel. The rest of me family think she's a cold-hearted bitch. But I know she's a wonderful actress and she plays that role so well.

'No,' I say. 'Something I have to do, you know?'

'Let's get this woman to bed then,' Aunty Cora says, guiding me Ma up the stairs. Grace helps Kevin clean up the dishes from earlier.

My eyes track to the living room. The light is haunting. The coffin shadows cascade over his skinny face. I'm expecting him to sit up any minute now. Is this really a good idea? My eyes then find the whiskey on the table. That would help.

'You don't have to do this,' Aunt Catherine says.

She's sitting beside me now, polishing off the rest of her drink. Her cold hand rests on mine.

'You owe him nothing,' she adds.

'I owe you everything,' I say. I keep my voice low because Kevin has resentment for Aunt Catherine.

'This is something I have to do. Not for him. But for…' I point at the ceiling.

'I hope you mean your Mother and have not gotten religious on me.'

I scoff and chuckle.

A soft and warm woman with freezing-cold hands.

6

Whiskey is the drink of gods. Even better than the monarch known as coffee. I could write love songs about whiskey that some swampy blues band would probably sing. The amber fire warms the lining of my oesophagus and keeps me flushed in this cold room. I guess we have to keep the window open so he doesn't melt.

I dig out me phone and flick through some TikToks. A thought plops into me head and I type "David Dowling Time Traveller" into the search bar, for the laugh. I see the same video that little shit showed me earlier. What was his name? That's right, Killian with a fucking "K".

'You're not gonna believe who's a time traveller?' The video says. 'Bestselling author David Dowling from Dublin was born in 1985 but is shown in this footage in 1990 as a fully grown adult. Watch.'

I kill that and look up that little shite Killian. He has a new post.

'D'ya know who's a prick?' Killian says, speaking directly into the camera. He's walking in the video. It must have been directly after he left the house this morning. As he speaks, the text appears on the screen at the same time.

'That's right, local "hero" David Dowling.'

The camera then cuts to me earlier outside the front door. The camera shakes a little as I say, '*Are you taking the piss? It's me Da's wake today, and you're making fun of me?*'

The camera then cuts back to Killian, the little shit, as he continues his walking rant.

'*That's not how local celebs should act to fans. Shame on you, David. I'm offended.*'

Fucking hell! That little prick.

I check the comments. I know I shouldn't. These asshole trolls are going to back him up, call me an asshole or whatnot.

"*I don't even know why he's famous.*" The first comment says.

Great start. I don't know why I am either. Writers are usually overlooked unless you're Stephen King or J.K. Rowling.

"*He's a prick.*" Is the next comment.

Me or Killian. I'm not sure.

"*Overrated.*"

It gets worse.

"*Wow, reading David Dowling's latest book was like watching paint dry! I've never seen such a boring plot and one-dimensional characters. I'd rather stare at a blank wall for entertainment.*"

"*It's laughable how he thinks he's a literary genius. Newsflash: your writing is as cliché as it gets. Do us all a favour and retire already!*"

"*I wouldn't recommend his books to my worst enemy. Save yourself the agony and avoid anything he's ever written. Trust me, you're not missing out on anything worthwhile.*"

I'm about to close it when I see a comment.

"It's easy to criticise from behind a keyboard, but David has dedicated his life to crafting captivating stories. His books have touched the lives of countless readers, and that's a testament to their talent."

And then this:

"While constructive criticism is valid, let's not forget that David is also a human being with feelings. This guy just shoved a camera in his face when he recently lost his father, so maybe we could cut them some slack during this difficult time. Compassion goes a long way, folks."

Then there are a slew of comments telling me that they are sorry for my loss.

"RIP MR DOWLING!"

Why am I doing this? Is this a punishment? I drop the phone on the couch. Too much internet for one lifetime.

I should have let Kevin sit with him. I bet he wanted to. As for Paul? That fucker ran off and never came back. What's up his arse?

'Do you know what's wrong with him?' I ask the dead Da and wait for a response. 'Exactly. You were never good at giving advice, were yeh?'

Did he just frown at me? Na! A trick of the light.

Whiskey has this effect on me. It does two things. It makes me see things that are not really there and makes me very nostalgic and sometimes weepy. Whiskey made Da a terrorist—a violent one at that.

One morning, dear diary in my head, it was particularly bad. I must have been about ten. It was a Saturday morning. I know that because I came downstairs for the triple bill of Batman, the animated series Gargoyles and Ghostwriter. Saturday morning TV was the best. My belly ached for some Coco Pops and the added bonus of chocolate milk after you finish the processed rice.

Anyway, I came down the stairs that Saturday morning as quiet as a proverbial mouse. I heard arguing the night before, so I didn't want to wake the beast with noise. I went straight into the kitchen for my sugar-fix breakfast and noticed the empty bottle of whiskey on the table. This was nothing new. I gave it the kind of glance you'd give a dirty cup that someone forgot to clean.

I dumped the Coco Pops into a bowl and fetched the milk. I saw blood in the sink when I passed it—streaks of dried red on dirty plates. I told myself it was ketchup– lying because I didn't want to face up to reality.

Reality hit back very hard when I walked into the living room. It's the same living room I'm in right now.

She was on the sofa, head back, neck exposed. At first, I thought, why is Ma sleeping downstairs? I knew she liked whiskey, but I never remembered her being drunk enough not to go to bed. Do you know that surge of dread that fills your stomach and floods your socks with sweat? I felt that, that day. I thought I had just walked in on my dead mother. It took me forever to get the courage to step up to her. When I did, I got such a fright.

Her face…

Her left eye was so swollen that I couldn't see her eyebrow anymore. It was like someone shoved a plum under her eyelid. Her cheek had a dried gash. That's where the blood came from, I guess.

There was fucking blood on the couch that had turned that dark brown colour.

The visuals didn't get me. It was her actions when I woke her that got me. Here was this lioness, a strong and powerful protector, gasping for air. She looked so frail and helpless, and when she finally came to her senses and realised I was standing in front of her, she panicked, as any mother would. I wasn't supposed to see this. This was personal. This was private.

She screamed at me to go back to bed.

I cried. An impulse, I guess. I thought, in my ten-year-old head, that she thought I did this to her in her sleep. I wanted to say sorry, that I didn't do it, but she wouldn't let me talk. She screamed at me again to get out. But the words felt weak. Pleading almost.

I ran upstairs and didn't open the door again. Paul was awake by then. He went downstairs and called for Kevin to hurry up and help. I didn't go. I stayed there the whole day. I heard me Da get up out of bed. I heard and saw the ambulance through the window. They took my Ma to the hospital—my Da went with her. Probably to make sure she didn't say anything.

I stayed in that room the whole day. I heard my Da come back from the hospital and beat Kevin for calling the ambulance. His cries for help made me feel queasy. I heard Da say, 'If I go to prison for this, I'm going to tell them that you helped me. You're coming with me.'

Da would plant seeds for me to hate Kevin at a very early age. I know now that Kevin didn't do anything but my brain back then hated him for it. My Da took that love away, that love for my brother. He also took away the image of my protector. I didn't want to see her when she came home the next day with a black eye, two stitches and broken ribs. I stayed in me room. I was so fucking hungry, but I didn't want to see her. I know now that all she probably wanted was a hug and cuddle from her little man, but I was punishing her for frightening me. All she wanted was love.

***

I wipe tears from my cheeks and stare at the coffin. It's just pieces of wood with a wax statue in it. All the power was gone from that man.

I pour myself another drink, and the urge to piss comes over me. I'm in the toilet at the top of the stairs, relieving myself, when I hear a thump coming from the living room. I literally stop pissing to listen closer. Satisfied that no one is downstairs, I finish taking a leak and wash me hands. I hear another thump.

My mind goes straight to that TikTok Killian. Is he back to fuck with me? I turn off the faucet and creep downstairs to try and catch the cunt in the act. I open the front door quietly and stick my head out. If he's here, I'll kill him.

Of course, there's no one there. Why would there be? The whiskey is taking control of me. I close the door and turn around to catch the fright of me life. Me Ma is standing behind me in a dressing gown.

'What the fuck are you doing?' she says with puffy eyes and a bedhead.

'I thought I heard something outside?' I slur.

'Jesus, Mary and Joseph, you're drunk.'

'Yeh'd have to be, wouldn't yeh?' I say, nodding at the coffin through the living room door.

'Let's get you to bed, son.'

Ma leads me to the couch. I slump down for the night. It's amazing what a bit of fresh air can do. I went from being grand to dead drunk in seconds.

'Are you sure you're okay?' she says to me after fetching a blanket.

'Ma?'

'Yes, son?'

'Are you relieved? Seriously now.'

'Your Dad was a sick man.'

'Whaddaya mean?'

'If he grew up now, he would have gotten the treatment. But…' she trails off. Secrets are rampant in this house.

'Are you saying he was…' I point to me head, screwing my finger on my temple.

'I'm saying, go to sleep.'

She kisses me on the forehead and goes to bed.

***

I drift. Not asleep, but not fully awake. I'm somewhere in between. I can feel the shift in the air. A heaviness sits upon me, and I try to open my eyes. When I do, he is standing in front of me, erect, skinny and in silhouette. He cracks his arms out, reaching for me. I turn my cheek to him. Declan Macy's voice runs through my head in reverb. *"The night before a funeral is when you see shit....You'll see tonight. The soul or whatever you want to call it. It rebels."*

It rebels.

I open my eyes.

He's sitting beside me.

His face gaunt.

His breath shallow.

He's staring at the corner of the living room ceiling. I try to scream, but nothing comes out. I turn my head to face away from him, only to find the younger version of him standing in front of me.

He's up in my face. Real close. His breath smells of rotting flesh.

'Do you see,' younger Da says.

7

I had the weirdest dream about Da. I dreamt I was in a bar with him. He was much younger, and I was me, David, but I wasn't. You know how dreams are. I didn't recognise the setting, but it was a bar with many drinkers. A small group of men were laughing and having a good time. Then, in walks this woman.

She is young. Too young to be in the bar. Da watches her cross the pub and order a drink. Da smiles at her when she looks around.

Then, the dream transitions to the toilets. Da is in the cubicle with the girl while I look in the mirror, washing my hands. The girl starts to scream, but not in pleasure. I turn my attention to the cubical and begin to kick it in. When the lock gives away, I push open the door to find the girl holding a brand new baby. There is blood everywhere, far too much for anyone to survive.

A child giggles behind me, and I spin around, trying to catch the rascal in the act. The kid runs out of the toilets, and I try to follow.

Then, all of a sudden, I'm in the city centre, and the kid runs up to my Da. It's a girl. The kid hugs Da. He turns to me and says, 'Do you see?'

***

Kevin is standing over me. It's morning, just about. He has a cup of coffee in his hand, and my neck aches from sleeping upright all night.

'Smell of farts and whiskey,' he says.

'Are you sure it's not him,' I say. 'Saw him walking around last night.'

'That's not even funny.' Kevin hands me the coffee. The first nice thing he has done so far.

'He sat right there,' I say, pointing at the empty space beside me. 'And looked into that corner. Fucking trippy.'

'Get up and get showered. The funeral home will be over soon.'

I stand. Knock back the coffee and try to stretch out my tight neck. That's when I see it. Pinned to the inside of the coffin, just sticking out of the fabric, is the corner of an envelope.

'What's that?' I say to Kevin.

He follows my finger and fishes the envelope out of the coffin.

'I guess people leave stuff in the coffin.' Kevin opens the envelope and then looks at me. 'Did you write this?'

'What is it?' I say.

He takes out a postcard from the envelope. I can see that it's a Dublin City postcard. He spins it around so I can see the content written on it.

I'M GLAD YOU'RE DEAD.

'Jesus,' I say. 'That's a bit dark, even for me.'

'That's not even funny, David.'

'That wasn't me.'

'Who was it then?'

'Have you met our Da? It could have been anyone. Throw it in the bin.'

'That's fucking disgraceful,' Kevin says, walking into the kitchen.

'What is?' Ma says. She's making tea. We hadn't even noticed her coming down.

Kevin thinks fast. 'David's drinking.'

'Just for one day,' Ma starts- 'will yeh play a different feckin' record. Yes, your brother carries his Father's curse.'

– 'I don't have a drinking problem,' I add.

– 'But today is not the day for that conversation,' Ma continues.

Did Ma just defend me and call me out at the same time? She never does that.

'And you,' she says, pointing her twiggy finger at me. 'Get showered, you smell like a distillery.'

***

Declan Macy is in the living room when I come back down. He gives me a sideward glance as he lowers the coffin lid.

'Did his soul rebel?' he says with a smirk.

I return the smirk, 'I think so.'

'Want one last look?'

'No,' I say automatically.

His helper, or assistant as they might like to be called, fixes the hinges back onto the coffin. They had been removed last night for convenience's sake.

Something comes over me when they latch the coffin shut. Was it relief or melancholy or some sort of finality? It's the last time I'm going to see him.

My brain immediately jumps back in time. Bastarding whiskey is still in me system. I'm ten. I'm in the living room faking an illness, so I don't have to go and play football. Da wanted me to be a professional footballer. He said I had the talent but I never made the starting lineup. Ma was talking to me, telling me to say what was wrong with me because she knew I wasn't sick. A mother knows. I tell her I don't want to play football just as Da comes in the living room door. It's comical timing at its best.

'You fucking cunt! I begged them to take you on the team!' He growls at me.

He fucks a cup across the room, tea staining the wallpaper for months after.

***

I'm back in the same living room twenty-seven years later, staring at the closed veneered oak coffin with a plain-sided finish. Declan and his assistant disappear into the kitchen for some tea and biscuits.

I sense me Ma staring at me. Her eyes drilling into the back of me skull, trying to figure out what I'm thinking.

'Do you know why I don't want to have kids?' I say loud enough for her to hear but not the funeral director.

'You don't want to have kids?' Ma says. I can hear the heartbreak in her voice.

'I think there's too much of him in me.'

I can't see her, but I can tell she's holding her breath.

'I drink too much, like you said. I can't seem to hold a relationship down. They piss me off after a while.'

'I liked Nicole, she was nice,' Ma says; she's holding my hand now, taking a step to my side.

'Yeah? She was mad. Used to submerge her toothbrush in a glass of water overnight. Who does that?'

'I think a lot of people do.'

'That's fucking weird, Ma.'

Nicole was my last ex. A Brit working as an English teacher at an International School in Budapest. Funnily enough, we met in a bar and sparked up a conversation about Shakespeare's Hamlet, of all things. I tried to tell her that it was Claudius, the brother of King Hamlet, who was the main character in the play. Not Hamlet. As an English teacher, she was baffled by my observation. I told her he was a more interesting character because a man who kills his brother for the woman he loves deserves to be the main character. I won her heart with my wit and broke it when I realised I couldn't be sixty-five years old and still hold a conversation with her.

'You're not like your da,' Ma says to me. 'You actually remind me of my daddy. He had mad thoughts like you. Always good for a yarn too far-fetched to be true.' She turned my face with a cold hand. I stared into her soul as she says, 'But he was also kind, and gentle. A well read man. Could have written books like you, but God thought he was too good for his world.'

I see a tear rolling down her cheek. She's struggling with the next words.

'It's a shame you never met him,' is all she could get out. 'Excuse me.'

***

Paul and Martina are at the door ten minutes later. I'm drowning in coffee and ibuprofen, hoping that this hangover will piss off for a couple of hours. Paul gives me the cold shoulder when he comes into the kitchen. Martina shoots daggers from her eyes.

'What is wrong with you?' I ask without thinking. I didn't actually want to know what was wrong with him. I knew it was about money because it's always about money.

'Nothing,' he snapped.

He gave me an out not to continue the conversation. Kevin comes in, checking his combed hair in the oven glass as Paul brushes past him, joining the funeral director out back for a smoke.

'What's his problem,' Kevin asks me.

I shrug me shoulders. 'I don't remember saying anything bad last night to him. He stormed off after he said he was transferring money to me.'

'He has money?' Kevin quips.

'You're a bunch of bastards. Heartless, heartless bastards,' Martina snarls.

I tilt me head to see that she has tears in her eyes. Am I missing something important?

Martina slams the door on the way out of the house.

I look at Kevin. It's his turn to shrug. My attention turns to Paul out the back window. What was going on? Should I care? If I ask, I know I'll get annoyed.

'Are we ready?' Ma asks from the hallway.

Declan Macy moves through the kitchen. 'Right lads. It's time.'

***

The ride to the church took ages. Declan Macy must have been driving five kilometres an hour. I know Finglas isn't that big of a town, but Jesus, I've had shorter relationships than this journey. Ma is beside me in the car. Paul and Martina are in the back, and Kevin is up front with Declan. Ma looks pale. The bags under her eyes have grown since we got in the car. It might be the journey that aged her. Paul and Martina are whispering in the back. I'm trying not to listen.

I see the occasional pedestrians bless themselves as we pass them. It's such an odd thing, religion. Was their blessing going to get Da into heaven? Maybe it's like coupons. If he got enough blessings on the way to the oven, he might get to the Pearly Gates.

***

The funeral car finally pulls up outside the church. The tiniest church in Finglas. There's a splattering of people outside, all dressed to code. I spot Uncle John beside the entrance, laughing it up with some of his chums. My aunts are giving him the widest berth. They huddle together like a pack of wolves waiting to feast on any person who will disturb their sister's mourning. Beside them is Uncle Pat, my mother's brother. I'm actually surprised to see him. He's a recluse by nature, only leaving his home for work and food. Doesn't drink, doesn't smoke. He's well-respected because he doesn't talk much; however, people seem to listen when he does. That's how I remember him anyway.

I help Ma out of the car and walk her to the top of the aisle. Declan Macy wheels the coffin in front of us, and the altar boys, two teenagers with stupid, identical Dublin haircuts, help place the flowers on top. Some melancholy country song plays over the PA as Ma greets the priest. He's a bearded man who had a gut built out of beer and red meat. He says a few words to her, offers her a front-row seat and turns to me.

'Are you the son?' the priest says. He's a country boy. Somewhere southwest of Ireland.

'I am. One of three.'

'Are you the writer?'

'I am.'

He looks left and right, lowering his tone before continuing.

'I might have a few, er, books for you to sign later, if you don't mind?'

This lad has some gallstones. On the day of me da's funeral, of all days, he wants me to sign copies of me books. I'm taken aback and a little humble at the same time.

I nod me head at him.

'Love your work.'

'You too, Father.'

Why did I say that?

The priest gestures to the front row beside Ma. She leans in after I sit.

'What did he want?' she whispers.

'For me to sign copies of me books for him.'

'What the actual...' she starts, then remembers she's in the house of God. She blesses herself just in case God hears her thoughts.

Kevin sits beside me. He stares up at the priest as he takes position at the pulpit. The priest waits until the country song is finished. I'm not even sure Da liked country music. Ma does. Seems like a strange choice of music until I listen to the lyrics. *'Eeeeeeii fallll to pieeeecessss, each time someone speaks your name , I fall to pieces, Time only adds to the flame.'*

Was she trying to tell us something? Who knows. Mothers are the ultimate crossword challenge that only 1% of the world can figure out.

The priest taps the microphone with a lot of reverb behind it.

'In the name of the Father, and of the Son and of the Holy Spirit. The grace and peace of God the Father, and the love of God, and the fellowship of the Holy Spirit be with you all.'

The whole church erupts in a chorus of, 'Amen.'

I'm surprised that people can coordinate like that these days. I'm staring at the priest's white poncho-like robe, and my writer's brain kicks in. I'm wondering what temperature he washes it at. Would it be a boil wash? Does he use bleach to get it snow-white?

'Ma,' I whisper, 'Do you think he washes that at 60 degrees or?'

Ma cranes her neck at me. 'What is wrong with you?'

'God heard that.'

She blesses herself again.

I feel a hand on top of mine. I look down to see that it's Kevin with a note. I take it.

'Good morning, everyone, and welcome to our funeral mass, which we offer for the happy repose of the soul of Brian Dowling, who died last Monday, and now we gather to remember his life and commend him to our loving God,' the priest says.

I stop listening and concentrate on the note. This is unusual for Kevin. First, he stuck up for me with Uncle John, and then he was kind to me this morning. If this is a note that says he loves me, I'm going to cry rivers.

I unfold the paper and take a peek at its contents. I feel like I'm back at school doing something terribly naughty. I hope Santa is not looking.

YOU'RE DOING THE EULOGY!

My heart does a double beat. It could be the whiskey passing through it or the fucking shock of it. I look at Kevin. He's staring at the priest, but there's a smirk on his face. A "Gotcha" smile.

'We will begin our service with symbolic acts, and the first thing we will do now is to light four candles. We will light them with the Easter candle that stays lit all year round as a remembrance of Jesus's suffering. The four candles will be lit by Grace, Cora, Catherine and Pat,' the priest says and waits for Ma's siblings to transfer fire from one thick candle to four small candles.

I'm not really paying attention to him. I'm panicking. What should I say? I place my lips up to Kevin's ear.

'Are you joking?' I say. No response. 'Are you joking?'

This time, he shakes his head. Never once looking at me.

My breath is out of control. Palms flood with sweat. I'm watching Pat light a candle, but I can't remember why he's doing it. When is the eulogy part of a funeral? Is it at the beginning or the end? Shite. I have no idea what to say. Do I lie? "Brian Dowling was a loving man?"

Fuck.

I think I'm having a panic attack. Words are not lining up the way they should. I'm struggling to find fragments of coherent words.

Uncle John is placing a bible on the coffin. Paul is behind him with a picture of Da in his prime. He was a handsome man. Old-timey Hollywood handsome. Like that fella from Psycho. What's his name… Perkins. What is going on? I'm losing track. I should be concentrating on what to say.

Fuck.

I'm going to beat the shit out of Kevin when this is finished. He can join me da, in the crematorium.

'As we gather at this sad time for Brian's family,' the priest says. 'We extend our condolences to his children Kevin, Paul and David. To his brother John. To his sister-in-laws, brother-in-laws—'

I stop listening to the priest. All I can hear is high frequencies. My left ear is playing drum and bass. It has to be my heart. I write words down. I don't say them. *Brian is, was… a man.*

Fuck.

I check back in with the funeral. The priest is talking about God. That's good. priests usually talk about him for a while.

'And now, Brian's son, David will say a few words about his father, Brian.'

My legs won't work. Someone replaced my bones and muscles with strawberry jelly. Ma looks at me, surprised. Then her face lit up, thinking that I had changed my mind. I haven't got the heart to cause a scene now. I want to, don't get me wrong. I want to do that part in the romcom movie where they cause a fuss in a church. "Don't *marry him, have me.*" Or, in my case, "I'm *not doing it. It's Kevin's job. He's the eldest.*"

I drag my feet to the altar. All eyes are on me. I look up at the crowd of mourners. All waiting patiently for me to say something, anything. I spot Linda. She gives me a smile that I remember from adolescence. My chest feels warm. That's exactly what I needed.

There is someone I don't recognise at the back of the Church. She's a redhead in a brown leather jacket and blue jeans, about my age. There is something about her that sparks a memory but I can't place her. I blur her out of my view and concentrate on Linda.

I tap the mic. It's obligatory. I clear me throat.

'Erm…'

8

The winter air soothes my rosy cheeks. I'm outside of the church, dying for a smoke. People are congratulating me on the speech. I know they're just trying to be polite. I fumble in my pockets for my pack of smokes. I can't find them. Shite. My eyes scan the crowd of black jackets, trying to spot a smoker. I'm trying not to make eye contact with Ma or anyone from the immediate family. Two cigarettes sticking out of a pack in front of my face. Linda Murphy to the rescue.

I take one and light up. 'Thanks.'

'That was… a bold move,' she says.

I look to her for comfort. 'How bad was it?'

'I thought it was… what's the right word to say… fair.'

'Fair was the word you were scrambling for.'

'It was the nice version. You didn't lie, but you didn't tell the whole truth either. You were…fair.'

I feel a firm hand wrap around the back of my neck. Uncle John's face is up to my ear. His teeth clenched as he grunts, 'The fuck did you say about me in your speech?'

I jerk out of his grip. 'The fuck away from me.'

Linda places an arm between us. 'Leave it out, lads.'

Eyes have fallen on us.

'You've some fucking balls. Ya little pup,' he barks at me.

'Do you think I'm afraid of you, big man,' I say. I'm shitting bricks, but I try to keep my voice intact.

'You fucking will be,' he says, squaring up to me. Linda is trying her best to shove him off, but she's only a stick of a woman.

'John Dowling!' Ma shouts from the crowd.

He turns enough to catch her eye. She's standing among a mob of mourners. Her face was distorted with resentment. 'You will not cause a scene on the day of your brother's funeral!'

'Did ya not hear what he said?' John asked. I could feel the anger radiating from his body.

Onlookers began to whisper. My Ma took a solemn step forward. 'My son placed a mirror up with his words today. It was your choice to look at it and not like what you see.'

Jaysus, me ma spitting out the truth like she's Oscar Wilde.

'But it's all a bunch of–' John began.

–'Don't say "lies". My son wouldn't lie in the house of God,' she cut in.

Ma knows I'm an atheist. She doesn't accept it, but she knows it.

John does this thing that kids with tantrums do. He boils up all his frustration into a loud screech before storming off to his BMW. I return my gaze to Ma, who isn't looking at me. She heads to the funeral car. It will be a long silent ride to the cemetery. I might have messed this up, and I know who to blame.

#

I couldn't find him anywhere, the prick. Kevin wasn't in the car on the way to the cemetery for the cremation part of the ceremony. Ma didn't say a word to me the whole trip– I knew that would happen. I know she was annoyed at me because she was talking nicely to Martina. Paul was giving me the cold shoulder, too.

I want to get on a plane and piss off home. I can be home by midnight if I get the evening flight to Vienna and then get the train from there. All direct flights are in the morning time. Maybe I'll stay in Vienna for a few days. Soak in some opera and have a Schnitzel. That might cheer me up.

We pull into Glasnevin Cemetery, stopping outside of the second chapel of the day. That's when I spot that woman. The one with the leather jacket. I ask Ma, 'Who's that?'

She ignores me. Drives me nuts about this family. Instead of speaking their minds, they decide to ignore things that bother them. If they stay quiet, it will go away. It's a defence mechanism to counter Brian Dowling's wrath if you ever spoke your mind.

***

My mind goes to that time. That one time, I spoke out. I broke the mould. Seventeen, I was. It was Friday, and he was drunk.

He was picking on Ma about the coldness of his dinner. She was trying to explain to him that the microwave was on the fritz and she couldn't afford a new one. I'm trying to get my homework done so I can go to Linda's place. Her mam and dad were going out, and she'd have a free gaff for fooling around.

'Why can't you just make me a fresh dinner when I get in?' he asks. His voice is always in a state of annoyance.

'Dinner is at six o'clock. If you can't make it home on time, then you have to deal with the shitty microwave. Or you can stop drinking and pay for a new one?'

'I work fucking hard all week,' he starts. He's like a snake coiling up, ready to strike or, in his case, come out swinging.

I stop writing but keep my head down. We are a well oiled machine, the Dowlings. We know what's coming and slip into our little blankets of comfort embedded deep in our subconscious. I'm searching for mine as Da stands to get up real close to Ma. Close enough for her to get the meaning of his rant.

'Do you not think I deserve to blow off a little steam? Would you prefer I blow off some steam here?' he says.

'Please, Brian,' Ma says. But it's the way she says it. Like an animal who knows it's trapped and might not see the dawn of a new day.

He moves closer, pinning her to the kitchen sink. His crotch presses into her hip as she tries to turn away from him.

'Are you not grateful that I release all that anger somewhere else? Do you want it here, in this kitchen, May?' His big digger hands wrap around her chin. 'Would you prefer that?'

I can't find my comfort blanket. It is replaced with a small glowing orb of hate. It grows with every word that man says. I can't control its growth. It's out of control.

'How about you make me a fresh fucking dinner,' he screams in Ma's face.

'How about!' I bellow. 'You take your fucking hands off her.'

Da stops, gobsmacked. He turns around, releasing Ma as he does. I'm in his crosshairs now. At least it's not her.

That ball of anger is seeping through my tendons. It's burning my nerve endings.

'What did you say?' he says in disbelief.

'You know what I said to you,' I say in a direct tone.

'Are you taking the piss?' he says. He edges closer to the kitchen table. I can see the bulge in his jeans. He loves this. It gets off on it.

I grip the ballpoint pen in one hand, relishing as the ball of anger breaks through my skin, cracking my voice as I say, 'Just leave her the fuck alone, will ya?'

'C'mer to me. Let me talk to you real close,' he says as he grabs one of my heavier textbooks. The kind he can place against my chest and punch so that it doesn't leave any marks on my body. I'm not going through that again.

'Back the fuck off,' I snap.

'Brian, please, leave him,' I hear Ma say. She doesn't move from the kitchen sink. She's afraid. Just like I should be, but I'm surprisingly not.

'Big man, are we?' Da slides up beside me. I'm standing now, back pressed against the wall. He shoves the textbook up to my chest and is about to put his shoulder into a punch when I swing at him with the ballpoint pen.

It lodges in his forearm. 'Fuck!' he recoils back, dropping the textbook. I immediately pick it up. A weapon.

'You're fucking dead!' he spits, pulling the pen out. Blood starts to gush. Ma gasps.

'Jesus, David, what did you do?' she squeals.

Da comes at me like a bull. I drop the shoulder and let him crash into the wall. Instinct tells me to swing the book, so I do. It connects with the back of his head. He's sluggish now from the blow and the alcohol. He swings his arms randomly at me. Two swings connect with my defending arms. He's strong.

Ma jumps in, trying to push him away from me. She gets thrown to the linoleum. Da comes at me again. I try and punch him, but I don't know how to throw a punch to save my life. I connect with his jaw, but it doesn't phase him. He connects with my chest, and I can't breathe. He's on top of me, one punch after another. Wack! Wack! I see stars, galaxies– the big bang. I'm gonna die.

I wake up in a hospital with my aunt Catherine sitting beside me. She says, 'You're going to rest up and then come stay with me for a little bit until everything calms down.'

That was the only fight I was ever in. I lost, and I never went home.

9

There are ghosts inside this chapel. I can tell. The chill I got when I walked in followed me to the front row. The wine-coloured carpets, matched with the decades-old pews, leave all comfort outside the cemetery gates. I don't understand the tradition of having a funeral mass in a church and then going to another chapel for more God talk before they take him away for cremation. It's all too much.

I turn around to see Uncle John sitting in the back of the chapel, arms folded like a sulking child. Behind him is that woman. The one in the leather. I'm about to ask Ma about her again when I feel a squeeze on my arm. It's Aunt Catherine. She leans in and gives me a sideward hug.

'I know that it was hard for you to say those things at the Mass. But I want you to know that I'm proud of you,' she says in her ever-calming voice.

'Listen, I never thanked you enough for everything you've done for me,' I tell her.

'I've done nothing but be present,' she says, but the squeeze of my arm says more.

'Was the speech bad?'

'Not your best work,' she says before adding, 'Don't take it out on your brother. His hell is over now and he doesn't know what to do with his freedom.'

Jesus! Poets are rampant in my family.

'Who's the woman in the leather jacket?' I ask. 'The one at the back of the chapel.'

Aunt Catherine spins around in the pew but is distracted when the priest stands beside Da's coffin.

The congregation blesses themselves again and listens to the final stretch of the funeral procession. My eyes fall on the coffin, trying to think if there are any happy memories.

Any.

Did I block them all out? Fortify them behind impenetrable walls? I'm in a daze, searching door after door in a corridor of memories. I see him at Christmas, preparing the dinner. The only time he ever made food for his family. I remember him with a Guinness moustache, giggling at something my ma said. Chris Rea is singing about driving home for Christmas in the background. I witness Da spooning a colossal dollop of mashed potatoes out of the plastic bowl and plopping it on Ma's nose. Paul and Kevin are killing themselves laughing. Da leans in, wraps his mouth around Ma's nose, and the mash disappears.

Another memory door opens, and I'm in a cinema. I'm really young. I'm too young to be watching *Who Framed Roger Rabbit*. I'm looking up but can barely see over the seat in front of me. I'm missing the last third of the screen. I hear my Da bellowing with laughter. The whole row of chairs shake with the force of this man. Popcorn bubbling like an earthquake out of the box.

He looks down at me. 'Funny, isn't it?'

I don't see Paul or Kevin this time. We must have been alone. Maybe I'm remembering it wrong. Or, maybe I want to remember it like this.

***

The priest's voice cuts through memory lane. 'Our brother Brian Dowling has gone to his rest in the peace of Christ. May the Lord now welcome him to the table of God's children in Heaven. With faith and hope in eternal life, let us assist him with our prayers. Let us pray to the Lord also for ourselves. May we, who mourn, be reunited one day with our brother.'

There have to have been moments of pure bliss. There has to be something other than fear. I need to believe that. A man can't just be one colour. Nothing is that absolute. A birthday, a holiday, something. A wave of guilt tackles me. Were we that bad? Was it us that made him miserable? Did he not want us? Were the three pregnancies the anchor that lodged him into a marriage that kept him from his dreams? Did he have dreams? What the fuck did he want to do when he grew up? It definitely wasn't a labourer. Did he want to be a footballer? Is that why he pressured me into doing it? He wanted to live vicariously through me? That's no way to live.

I'm brought back to the world with Ma squeezing my hand. She hands me a tissue. I didn't realise I was crying. I wasn't crying for him. I was crying for the man he wanted to be. The man who had a path he wanted to take and a path he was forced down. A path he resented and fought and bruised and battered.

I wipe my eyes and listen to the priest, 'Because God has chosen to call our brother Brian from this life to himself, we commit his body to be cremated, for we are dust and unto dust we shall return.'

I feel the lifeblood in myself draining. A passage in the memoirs is finally finished. Time to command-enter to the next page and type in the new chapter. The priest steps forward.

'With longing for the coming of God's kingdom, let us pray: Our Father, who art in   Heaven, hallowed be thy name.'

The chapel took on a murmur of the Lord's Prayer. A prayer beat into us in primary school. Christ, we had to ream that baby off like it was tattooed to yer brain. I bet you continued the following line after *hallowed be thy name*.

With the unison of 'Amen', the Mass ended.

That was it.

Declan Macy and his assistant wheeled the coffin behind a curtain, never to be seen again. The priest then left us in silence. We just sat there, not knowing what to do now. There's a random cough that seems obligatory for a funeral. Ma was the first to stand. She was our key to getting the fuck out here. She suddenly stops and turns to me.

'How much money do you have on you?' she asks.

'Why?'

'We need to pay the priest,' she says.

'We need to pay the priest? Does Rome not pay him?'

'Give him fifty.'

'Jaysus.'

She walks out of the cemetery chapel and everyone follows suit.

***

I catch up with the priest at the back of the chapel as he dumps his robes into the boot of his car. He stretches his back, trying to crack it back a couple of decades.

'There you are, David,' he says without seeing me. It must be a perk to being a man of cloth. God has his back.

'Now Father. I have something for you just to thank you for your wonderful service.'

I open my wallet only to find a hundred euro note. Nothing else. Bollix.

I hand it over. 'Sorry, we don't have an envelope. Bit of a hectic morning.'

'Not to worry,' he says, taking my hundred euros. 'Were you watching the match last night, David?'

'No, Father, I was watching me da.'

'I see. You were the one with him all night?'

'I was.'

'Did he rebel?'

'Why do people keep saying that?' My conversation was finished as soon as I lost a hundred quid. 'Anyway, Father. Have a–'

'Are you forgetting something, David?'

I'm baffled. 'I'm not sure. Have we to say a prayer?'

The priest chuckles. 'Good one.'

He then disappears into the boot of his car and returns with six of my books.

'Ah yeah,' I say.

He hands me the battle-worn paperbacks. I take his pen and sign the copies for him.

'Do I make them out to you, Father?'

'Er, could you make them out to Ashling?'

Who the hell is Ashling must have been plastered on my face.

'She's my sister,' he says quickly. 'Huge fan of yours. We both are.'

That's a relief. I have visions of the priest breaking his vow of celibacy. Visions I shouldn't have conjured up.

'That's very kind of you.'

'I'd ask you where you get your ideas from, but as I wander around the parish, I see your books everywhere.'

'I don't get ya, Father.'

'Sure, Finglas is in all of your books. Your characters are the people I meet every day. The zombies in the latest ones are the yobos that spend all their money on a holiday just to ruin everyone else's summer. The mother in Greenroom is every struggling mother in Finglas. She's like my mother, God rest her soul.'

'That's nice to hear, Father. Thank you.'

It was time to boogie out of there. I hate it when people wrongly interpret my work and think they know me. Fuck that. The Zombies are fucking Zombies, and the mother in Greenroom is my Aunt Catherine. I won't tell anyone that. She knows it. That's all. She took me in at a tipping point in my life. I could have gone one way and become a labourer like the old man or be the man I wanted to be. She helped me write my first screenplay when I left the hospital. I thought I wanted to be this Hollywood hotshot. But after the effort of having that movie made, I realised prose writing was my way to go. It took three novels to finally get published, and now I'm six novels into my career. All thanks to her.

***

On the way back to the gathering crowd outside the chapel, I see that woman again. She's walking away from the group about twenty feet away from me. It would bother the shit out of me if I didn't at least ask who she was to my Da. It's not like he had friends the same age as his sons. Maybe she was the daughter of a friend who couldn't make it.

'Excuse me?' I call.

I know she hears me, but she doesn't turn around.

'Excuse me, miss?' I call again.

'Leave me alone.'

I do a quick jog to catch up with her.

'I saw you at the funeral,' I say.

'Congratulations, you have eyes.'

'And just now at the chapel. How did you know my Da?'

'Go back to your family,' she says, quickening her pace.

'I'm just curious,' I say, agitated.

'Piss off,' she spits and takes off like I'm harassing her.

I stop following. 'You don't have to be a cunt about it, ' I muttered.

I watch her go, waiting for a reaction. I got none.

What the fuck was her problem?

10

I decide to ditch the crowd and walk through the cemetery to the official wake at the Botanic House Bar. As I wander through the pathways of Glasnevin, it was impossible not to feel the weight of history all around. The tombstones, weathered by the elements, carry stories etched in stone. One notable figure whose grave catches my attention is that of Daniel O'Connell, "The Liberator". His imposing round-tower monument stands as a testament to the man. I wonder if his da was nice to him, or was he a cunt?

Walking further, I fall upon the graves of some literary figures. Brendan Behan's tombstone has a hole cut out in the middle. An empty pint of Guinness is strategically placed inside. I found Christy Brown, too, *"Christy, Author and Artist."*

As I meander through the paths, the graves also tell tales of everyday folks. I can feel their struggles by looking at the graves where parents buried their children. The place has this quiet beauty, like a dance with life and death all at once. There is no smell of bleach and plastic here. Just earth and dying flowers.

Coming out of the cemetery, I find myself outside of the Gravediggers Bar. The old iron gates lead me straight to a bit of Dublin charm. With all its history and character, the pub practically invited me for a pint. I know I shouldn't, but I rarely get a chance to visit these places.

***

I find a spot at the battle-worn bar. Side palms have worn out the protective wax on the wood. How many would have sat right here beside the frosted glass partition that leads into the fireplace corner of the room? Hundreds? Thousands? A million? Old ale pumps stand sentry before me. I wonder, do they still work?

Why am I being so fucking melancholic?

Get a fucking pint in.

The barman takes my order for a dark creamy pint and I drink in the atmosphere. It's musty. An old Barfly gives me a nod. He has this mad patch over one eye. A Cyclops Barfly.

'How's it going?' I say. Maybe he'll spark up a conversation. I wrote a book about a bar and the conversations within. There was even a murder plot. Sure, you know all that if you're reading this.

'At a funeral, were yeh?' the Barfly asks.

He wears a farmer's cap with a matching tweed jacket. The Irish Independent paper folded over the bar. I look at his pint. It's a Smithwicks.

'Yeah,' I say. 'Me da's.'

The barman returns with my pint. 'Sorry for your troubles,' he says in passing. I pay with card.

'Get a lot of funerals in here, do yeh?' I ask the Barfly.

'One or two,' Barfly says with a pinch of sarcasm.

'At least the pint's good,' I tell him after my first giant gulp. I wipe the creamy leftovers off my top lip.

"Tis,' Barfly says before fixing his eye patch and tasting his own pint for the fifth time.

Our conversation drifts into the ether, and I hear the murmur and splatter of words vibrate off the pub's walls. Once or twice, sentences cut through like, 'Are yeh serious?' or 'Ah Jaysus, an awful shame that was.' You can tell this place has been around for ages by the short ceilings and beat-up wooden floors. Thousands of feet, if not millions. They've seen more than a century of spilt Guinness, piss and blood. Behind me is a spot where ladies used to have their own drinking space away from the lads – they've kept it like that to keep the old vibe, but honestly, anyone can use it now.

'Was your dad old?' Barfly turns to me. I can see a fresh scar poking out from under his patch.

'In his seventies.'

'Heart attack?'

'Stomach cancer.'

'Jesus.'

'I know, terrible way to go,' I tell him.

'I'll say a prayer for him tonight.'

'You don't have to,' I say. 'You didn't know the man.'

'True,' the Barfly says, 'but every man needs a prayer. It's tough enough being a man out there.'

'Jaysus, don't let the women hear you say that. There'll be an uproar.'

'Don't get me started. My wife used to chastise me. She'd say, don't be praying for men. They cause all harm in this world. D'ya know what I'd say to that?' He baited.

'Go on—'

'Sure, I'd say, behind every man is a strong-headed woman—nagging at him.'

He erupts with laughter. I don't get the joke. I think he's trying to play on, "behind every powerful man there's a strong woman," but sure, fuck it, I'll laugh along.

His laughter trails off into silence again. He frowns for a moment then shakes the frown away.

'She'll be dead three years next February.' He lets that sail momentarily before adding, 'Jesus Christ, I miss her.' His voice cracks at the end.

'Sorry for your loss.'

'She is a loss. Mother to my boy and my two girls. They miss her terribly also. They don't come around much. Too busy with their own lives.'

I'm immediately building a character from this Barfly. The lonely old man who sits by the fire after coming home from the Gravediggers. He visits his wife's grave every day. That's when I stop myself. Why not let him write his own character? Why not listen for once, David, instead of waiting for your turn to talk.

'Are they successful, or at least happy?' I ask and lean back on my stool.

'The boy is successful, yes. If that is a thing anymore. He works with computers at that Google place.'

I nod and let him continue.

'One of me girls is a lazy bitch. She has the talent but she loves procrastinating. Spent a fortune on college for nothing. My baby girl, she's happy. Found love against the word of the Bible. I stupidly mentioned that once— drunk. She doesn't talk to me now. Lives in America with her wife. My other daughter shows me pictures of her on Facebook. She looks happy. Honestly, happy.'

'Sorry about that,' I say.

'I say a prayer for her every night. I pray that she'll live a full life and that I'll meet her again in Heaven, give her a hug, and tell her I'm sorry.'

'Why not say it now?'

'Too much time has passed. Too much bad air. Too much resentment. I might as well be Sisyphus, rolling that boulder up the hill.'

I let the air breathe a bit.

'I bet she doesn't hate yeh,' I say.

'I'm not sure,' he replies.

'I just cremated a horrible bastard of a father. I know bad dads when I see them. They don't regret the words they say…I bet she'll see that. If you try adding her on Facebook, I bet she'll accept the friend request. And I bet if you write, "Hi, how are ya?"… She'll reply.'

He grunts.

'I know bad fathers. Trust me,' I finish.

'I don't even have Facebook,' he says, a hint of enthusiasm in his voice.

'Get your lazy daughter to help you. She's not doing anything. And here,' I say, drowning the end of my pint, 'if you get Facebook, add me as a friend and tell me how it went.'

'I would if I knew your name,' he says.

'David Dowling.'

I see him jotting the name down on the margin of his newspaper.

'The writer?' the barman asks as he collects my empty glass.

'The very one.'

'They say your last book wasn't great,' the barman says.

'They're a bunch of cunts.'

We all giggle, and I'm out the door.

11

I pick up some cash before heading down the road to the Botanic House, Bar and Restaurant. It's a lovely red-brick building. It says classic food and drink under the name. It better be; I'm starving.

I slip inside to the left bar and listen for the sound of the Dowling mourners. I can hear Aunt Cora's laugh coming from the back lounge. It sounds like a monkey sitting on a spinning washing machine. I follow the sound, passing green and wine-coloured stools that were sparsely occupied.

They are sitting at the back of the bar— in the restaurant area. It's split into two sections: a slightly elevated part with fine dining– Paul and Martina huddled in a corner. Below that, facing the bar is a long green leather bench with a splatter of high tables. That's where I see the Aunts, Ma and that prick, Kevin. There was no room for me, so I grab a leather-bound high stool at the bar. I order a Guinness and mind my own business. After my so-called eulogy, I still think bad blood might be in the air.

'I particularly liked the part where you called John Dowling a thug,' Uncle Pat says.

He sits down beside me, a glass of cola in his hand.

'Uncle Pat, Jesus,' I say. I lean in for a hug, but he backs away. I forgot. My reclusive uncle doesn't like to be touched. 'Sorry,' I add.

'Happens,' he says. 'So is everyone pissed at yeh?'

'Think so. Wasn't really prepared for the speech, kinda sprung on me.' My eyes turn to Kevin, laughing it up with his aunts.

'It appears that brothers can also be difficult,' he says.

'Must have been hard for you, growing up in a house full of girls.'

'I was the youngest. They looked after me until they couldn't.'

There was something sad in the way he spoke. I was supposed to read between the lines but not poke at the words.

'That's nice,' is all I could come up with.

'You know the saying, women marry their fathers… My sister May did. So I know how you feel. I wish I had the balls to say what you said at my own father's funeral. I wanted to thank you for that. Now that you said it, hundreds of sons can also speak freely about their abusive fathers.'

'Funny,' I say. 'Me Ma speaks highly of him.'

'She had selective eyes.'

Uncle Pat had a way with words. It was part of his upbringing. All the children were well-educated, they went to mass and joined evening clubs. They were the upper middle class. Their father, my grandfather, fancied himself a writer. Historical fantasies were his niche. I read a few manuscripts of his. They sell a bomb today but back then there was no market for that particular genre. He couldn't get published and took to the drink.

The Irish curse.

Whenever Catherine brought me along to visit her brother, I would always find myself lost in Pat's sitting room or parlour, as he would call it. He would have these massive bookshelves. Wall to wall. Not a TV in sight. Just two good armchairs, a couple of lamps and hundreds of hardback books. Most of which he inherited from my grandfather.

'Hardback is the way to go,' Pat would say to me.

He had one or two first-edition books that would be worth a fair amount of money in today's market. He said that they were his life insurance when he passes so his sisters could have a nice nest egg. I had to remind him that he was the youngest and most likely the last of his siblings to survive.

'Ah, then I'll leave it to you.'

I had asked Aunt Catherine back then why Pat was such a recluse. Maybe he had an accident or was attacked in the village or something. She had said that was a question to ask him when the time was right.

Sitting beside him at the bar in the Botanic House seems like that time.

'Can I ask you something, Pat?' I begin. 'Why'd you never get married?'

He takes a minute to formulate his words. 'You see, growing up the way I did,' he then stops, looks me in the eye and says, 'I don't have an answer for you.' With that, he goes and mingles.

Another victim of toxic masculinity. If our fathers don't challenge it, they risk passing on a harmful legacy that restricts emotions and keeps future generations trapped in outdated expectations. If my uncle is gay, why can't he say he's gay. If he's autistic, why couldn't he have gotten checked at an early age so he could live his life to its fullest potential? Why slap when you can hug.

I don't think my Da ever said 'I love you' sober. I never sat on the couch cuddling up to him, watching TV. I never danced to pop songs on a Saturday morning. The liquid I hold in my hand ruined my entire fucking life. Yes, I might be successful. Yes, I might be lying, saying that I'm not rich. But am I happy? I don't fucking know.

***

I'm now three drinks in and not an ounce of food to soak it up. Why am I doing this? The day is replaying in my head as I take a piss. I'm swaying. Jaysus.

I remember seeing that redhead in a brown leather jacket and blue jeans at the back of the church.

I remembered I was standing on the altar, looking out and there she was. I tapped the mic. It's obligatory. I cleared me throat.

'Erm…ladies and gentlemen, family and friends. Today, we gather here to remember and reflect on the life of Brian Dowling, a man who played a significant role in our lives. Brian was a father to three sons, Kevin, Paul, and myself. He was the husband of the most beautiful woman I've ever known. My mother, May. Brian's life was complex, marked by both, moments of joy, and challenges. It's important for us to acknowledge the reality of his struggles and the impact they had on those around him.'

That should have been the first sign to shut up. But I kept going.

'Brian faced battles within himself, and unfortunately, the difficulties he grappled with manifested in ways that affected his family. He was a father who loved his sons deeply but also struggled with inner demons that led to both mental and physical hardship for those closest to him. Today, we speak with honesty, recognising that his life, like any, was marked by imperfections. Growing up for Brian must have been hard. We could see traces of it still with the presence of his brother, John… a thug whose actions mirrored Brian's struggles, which must have come from an environment of turmoil and difficulty.'

There was an audible gasp at this point, I remember. I remember seeing my Ma's chin drop to her chest.

'In the face of adversity, we also remember the resilience and strength that defined Brian. As we reflect on his life, let us strive to break the cycles of pain and ensure that the lessons learned from his struggles contribute to the healing and growth of our family. May we find solace in the shared memories of both joy and sorrow, acknowledging that Brian, despite his flaws, played a significant role in shaping the lives of those he loved. As we say our farewells, let us focus on compassion and understanding, hoping that Brian has found peace in a place where the shadows of his internal pain no longer linger . In remembrance of Brian Dowling, let us cherish the positive moments, learn from the challenges, and strive for a future where love and understanding prevail. Thank you.'

Fuck. Did I really say that? No wonder why no one is talking to me.

***

I'm washing me hands, throwing laps of water onto my face. I need to sober up a little and get out of here. I think I missed the last plane of the day, but I can sleep at the airport. I need to quit drinking. I need to catch that demon and snuff it out. Hunt it down with a crossbow or an AK47.

But not tonight, no.

Tonight is the demon's send-off.

'Holy shit, you royally fucked it up, didn't yeh?'

His voice is like a rocket launch of anger. I see him standing at the toilet entrance through the mirror. I spin around to face Kevin. My father's rage coursing through my veins. I have him pressed up against the entrance. My forearm lodges up under his chin. My other hand gripping the wrist of his good arm.

'You fucking prick. Why would you put me in that position?'

'Because you, yeh bleedin gobeen couldn't keep your ego in check,' Kevin says and then sticks on a mocking voice, 'Oh, no Ma. I don't want to do the eulogy. I respectfully decline.'

'Why didn't you just fucking do it? I know you wanted to do it. I know you wanted to put him on this pedestal. A false idol to worship.' My teeth are gritting so much that they begin shooting warnings through my nerves.

'Worship? You are some man for one man. The writer couldn't miss an opportunity to talk about himself. All those words you said, it was all about you.'

I'm trying desperately to find a comeback. My arms are shaking with adrenaline.

'Why did you love him so much?' I shout. 'He used to beat the shit out of you. Out of us. He put Ma and me in the hospital, for fuck's sake!'

'I didn't love him!' he screams back. 'I loved the person I wanted him to be.'

There is this moment where we connect. We sync up for a split second and get each other. I release my grip as he says, 'I buried the father I wanted to have today. The loving kind. I know that's a lie, but you… buried a monster, and monsters have a way of coming back.'

I step back, slapped by his words and fall to the wet tiles. I'm not sure if it's water.

'I see it in you. His monster. It indulges in Guinness and whiskey. You're a fucking genius, but you're drinking your talents away. Do you even remember writing your last book?'

He's got me.

'I just don't want you finding a perfect woman like Ma and fuck it up because of what he did to us,' he says.

So we're having a heart-to-heart in the jax then, 'Turn the mirror around, son. Why haven't you found the perfect woman?' I say with a smile.

'I'm gay, you idiot.'

'Since when?'

'Birth.'

We have a little giggle. The tension settles like nuclear ash.

There's a bang on the door.

'What's going on in there?' Ma always knows when we're up to no good. We could see her tiny figure through the frosted glass.

'We're bonding,' Kevin says.

We giggle. I pick myself up off the ground and go to wash my hands.

All eyes are on us as we rejoin the party. Ma is standing at the bar where I was sitting. I'm in trouble. I'm thirty-seven and still scared of this woman. I swear she's getting older by the minute. I check my suit to make sure I'm presentable for her.

'Let's go for a smoke,' she says.

'You don't smoke.'

'But you do.'

***

Outside in the smoking area, I light one up, rejoicing in the hit of nicotine. Ma is standing beside me, her eyes looking up at me. From the corner of my eye, I can see her chest rise, pause and lower. The stop-start of "I want to say something."

'Jesus Ma, we'll be here all day.'

–'I'm disappointed in you,' she cuts in.

'In me?'

I know she is, but the teenager in me still comes out in the form of denial.

'You hung my sheets out. Now everyone knows what went on inside our house.'

–'I have a strong suspicion that they already knew.'

'That was private stuff, David. Private.'

'I didn't want to do the eulogy,' I'm saying this with some effort so it would get through to her. 'Fucking Kevin put me on the spot. So I spoke from my heart and you can't deny that.'

'David, Jesus Christ!' She looks to the heavens for answers. 'Give me a drag.'

She reaches for my cigarette and takes it. I remember years ago, my ma smoked. Everyone smoked back then. Seeing her smoke now looks odd and unbecoming.

'What you don't understand is that when you leave, I'm the one that people will look at and gossip about. I will become the– "Did ya hear?" You won't be around for that.'

'Do you really care what people think?'

'Yes, I do,' she says, raising her voice. 'Why do you think I hid it for so long? And you let the whole village know.'

'I'm sure the whole town knew it when your youngest was put in hospital and then sent away to live with his aunt.'

The air is sucked out of this smoking area. I'm in outer space, floating away from any sort of redemption from this conversation.

She doesn't say a word. She stomps the smoke in the ashtray and fetches her spare key from her bag. She waits until I take the keys before she turns on her heels and leaves.

'Ma?' I try calling.

Jesus Christ, how can one man fuck so much up in the space of a few days?

Kevin joins me after a minute.

'What's up with Ma?' He asks.

'She didn't like my words… again,' I say. Kevin has this look that wipes across his face, distorting it into a frown. 'I didn't upset her. She just didn't get her way.'

Kevin nods, not really believing me, but playing along.

'Right,' I say. 'Grab that drip of a brother of ours. This is my last night of drinking. We're taking the town until we can't walk any more. The monster is dead but let's drink to the da we wanted to have.'

'I can get behind that;' Kevin agrees.

'Then we can find out what's wrong with aul Paulie.'

12

You have to hand it to me ma. She has her ways to get back at me. Granted, it was a shit move on my part to throw the past in her face; however, leaving me with the bill for the Botanic House was a shit move on her part. All the meals and a round of drinks. I won't say how much it was but I will remember it.

The barman is fetching the visa card machine. I steal a look in Paul and Kevin's direction. They're in a deep discussion. Paul is not happy. Kevin is almost pleading with him. And, Martina? Martina is on her phone.

'Now sir, sign here,' the barman says and hands me the visa bill. I'm signing my name when I hear him say, 'Ah, Jaysus, Jenny. How are yeh?'

The Jenny in question says, 'Grand.'

When I look up, I see that Jenny is the redhead in the leather jacket. They say you can't smell vodka off someone's breath. That's a lie. She's had one or two. Maybe it's her eyes that have given it away. She's trying to focus on me but she doesn't know which eye to look at.

'You're back?' I say before she speaks.

She sucks the words she was about to say back in and presses her lips together. I ruined her mysterious entrance.

This is awkward.

She grunts before finally saying, 'You said I shouldn't be a cunt about it. So I won't.'

She leaves that statement hanging like sheets on a spring day.

'Okay…'

She's gulping too much. I hope she doesn't puke on me.

'You asked me if I knew your da. I did.'

'Ah yeah?' I'm paranoid that I'm about to meet his twenty-something-year-old mistress. I don't want to have that image in my head.

'Yeah,' she says. 'I also…'

I can see she's fighting the tears.

'You can just say it,' I tell her. 'Who am I to judge?'

'I also called him me da,' she blurts out. Realising what she said, she turns and runs out of the bar.

I go to follow her. 'What? Wait!'

'Hey!' the barman says. 'Your visa card.'

Fuck. I need that. I grab it off the barman and race out after her. Once outside, I scan the street, looking for her. Fuck. Nothing but red stone houses and traffic. She couldn't have gotten far, so I jog to the end of the Botanic Road. Nothing. Like a bleeding ninja she was.

When I get back to the Botanic House, Kevin and Paul are waiting. Martina is two steps behind them, watching traffic.

'What's going on?' Kevin asks.

'Have you ever seen that woman before?' I reply.

'Which one?' Paul asks.

'The fu– the fucking one I was chasing out of the bar, Paul.' I added the 'Paul' to prove I'm annoyed at his question.

'No,' he says. 'What did she look like?'

'Why the fuck did you say "no" if you didn't even see her?' Kevin asks.

Paul shrugs his shoulders.

'I saw her at the funeral,' Kevin says. 'And once outside Ma's house.'

'When was this?' I ask.

–'About two months ago after Ma took Da to the hospital.'

'Was she ringing the doorbell? Like, what was she doing?'

–'Just standing there. That's why I remember her.'

'Why?' Paul asks.

'She just said, in a roundabout way, that she's our sister,' I say and then correct myself. 'Half sister.'

'Fuck off!' Martina says with a high pitch.

'And you let her go?' Paul says.

I fold me eyebrows. 'Yes, I let her go. That's why I fuckin' ran after her down the street. Jesus Christ, Paul. I have been running since… I can't remember.'

'Ah, leave it out,' Kevin says, then adds, 'Doesn't surprise me. Not one bit.'

He looks like he took a punch to the chest. He's taking deep breaths.

'Did you at least get a name?' Paul asks.

'No.', I say, then remember. 'Wait!'

***

I barge back into the bar and find that bartender.

'C'mer,' I say. 'You called that lady Jenny.'

'Yeah, that's her name,' the barman says, wiping the counter.

'How do you know her?' Kevin asks.

'Jenny? She works in O'Neills in town.'

'Do you have like a contact for her?' Kevin says beside me.

'Sorry. Why do you need to know?' he asks.

'It's about our da,' Paul tells him.

'Maybe the pub would have her details.'

'Good man,' Kevin says. 'Thanks.'

We turn away from the bar. 'Jaysus, lads,' I say. 'This smells like an adventure.'

***

We jump in a taxi to O'Neill's pub on Suffolk Street. I remember meeting a date under the clock and heading in for a pint before going to the Savoy Cinema on O'Connell Street. She was gorgeous… fuck. What was her name?... Wendy.

Inside, I order the pints. A Guinness, two ciders for Paul and Martina– who insisted on tagging along, and a Bacardi coke for Kevin. Because he's different. They must have about thirty taps on the bar. All sorts of lager and ales and whatnot. The lads and

Martina are on the table behind me as I wait. Once I get the barman's attention, I ask, 'Do you know Jenny that works here?'

'I do,' he says and walks off.

I'm confused. I hear him say to someone around the corner of the bar. 'He's here.'

I expect to see Jenny. Instead, I see a bar lady with a book in her hand.

'Are you David?' she asks.

'That's me.'

She hands me the book and says. 'Jenny says to give you this and only this. No numbers, no address.'

'Seriously?'

'She made me promise. Good luck.'

She goes back to work and I look down at the book. The cover is familiar because it's mine. It's my second book, *"Cheers! Darling."* I toss it on the table and tell my gang what the barlady said.

Martina takes the book and examines it. 'It's your book.'

'Um-hm.'

'What does it mean?' she asks.

'I dunno.'

'Is there a number inside?' Kevin asks.

Marina flicks throughout the book, looking for pen scratchings or any other clue. She shakes her head in defeat.

I spin on my stool, trying to get the bar lady's attention. She spots me, raises her hands in the air and says, 'I don't know what else to tell yeah. That's all she said.'

We sit there for a while, stewing over Jenny— Jenny, our half-sister... maybe. She could be lying. But as Kevin said, he wouldn't put it past my da to have—

'Another family,' Paul says, reading my mind.

'She's not on socials,' Martina says, looking up from the glow of her screen.

'Thanks,' I say.

'Why'd she give us the book?' Kevin asks.

I look at the cover— an early paperback print of *Cheers! Darling*. This was the book that got me a Booker Prize and sent me into the bestseller lists, which in turn made my first book, *Greenroom*, also into a bestseller. *Cheers! Darling* was about a man on the eve of his wife's funeral, reenacting a Dublin pub crawl he went on with her on their first date. It was the new *PS, I Love You*. It was fresh, funny, and weird.

Pub crawl.... The cogs in my brain started to grind. I take the book in my hand and flick to the first pub on the crawl.

'Fuck me,' I say to myself. 'The first chapter!'

I spin the book around to reveal the title of the chapter: *O'Neills*.

Kevin cocks his head. 'Is she Da Vinci coding us?'

*'The night started in O'Neills. I was to meet her under the clock outside in the freezing cold. My cheeks and nose were numb as she turned the corner onto Suffolk Stree*t,' I read aloud.

'It's a clue!' Martina was suddenly animated.

'Oh course it's about you,' Paul half mutters.

'What happens in the pub?' Martina asks. At least she's not buried in her phone.

'Nothing. They have a drink and come up with a plan to visit all the spots where they had bad dates. That way if they have a good night, those places would have been exorcised. No more bad date demons.'

Paul mimics a microphone in his hand. 'Tell me something, David. Where do you get your ideas?' he says and shoves the imaginary mic into my face.

'You keep pushing, but I'm not letting you in. I've fought enough today.'

I hear Kevin whisper to him, 'What's gotten into you?'

Martina pounds back her cider. 'Well? Where to next?'

'What?'

'The book. Where's the second place on their journey?'

I flick the next chapter. 'O'Donoghue's, down the street.'

'Let's go!' she says with a ball of enthusiasm.

'Wait, babe, I haven't finished my drink,' Paul says. 'Anyway, this is David's game.'

'How is it David's game?' Kevin says. 'If it's true then she's our sister. Not David's'

'Yeah, but it's his book,' Paul continues.

—'So he wrote a fucking book! Whoop-dee-doo. He's done better than you. And it's not like you're a dumb cunt,' Kevin says. 'You're not. You got fucking honors in your leaving but instead of using yer brain you went with the easy option and went to work with the other minions in the construction. Yeh lazy prick! Don't shit on him because he did something. She's OUR FUCKING SISTER!'

Drinkers look in our direction.

I wipe a tear from my eye.

We're silent for a moment.

'Allegedly,' Martina says.

That was enough to get a chuckle from me. The lads relax. They have a way of doing that. I could have a fight with them and it would last for months until we forget what we were fighting about. But those two? They had this knack of just looking at each other and getting over it.

'Sorry,' Paul eventually says. The bottom of his eyes are welling up. Martina drops a hand down under the table to squeeze his leg.

'O'Donoghue's then,' I say.

I kill my pint and stand.

'Wait,' Kevin says. 'Why are we going to the next place? Why not just go to the last place in the book. That's where she is, right?'

My shoulders drop. I'm such a thick. Oh, of course, she'd be at the last pub. I open the last chapter. John Kavanagh's: The Gravediggers.

'I was there today already,' I tell them.

'And she wasn't there?' Martina asks.

'Unless she was in the fireplace section. I didn't check.'

'It is like an adventure,' Martina mutters.

'Back to the Gravediggers then.'

I turn around, ready for the door, when I spot the barlady who gave us the book. She's on the phone, giving us the side-eye. Something is not right. If it is a game, it's too easy.

I spin back around and flick through the book again. Halfway through, I stop. A chapter page is missing. Chapter 11. I try to think of the pub in question but can't remember. I start to read and realise it's The Foggy Dew.

'Okay detectives,' I say. 'We've found your next clue.'

13

It's a short walk to The Foggy Dew. Martina is giggling with excitement. I've never seen her like this before. Not that I know Martina. She's always been the one in the background, never causing a scene. Sometimes not even talking. Maybe that's why Ma doesn't like her. She would prefer a feisty woman for her boy. Paul said they had met at the Shelbourne races. She was there with her company having a three-course meal and watching the greyhound races as part of their Christmas bonus. Paul was…well, Paul was just there for the races. The legend goes that they struck up a conversation and met at Clery's clock the next night. For those of you who don't know, Clery's clock was the hot spot to meet dates before heading out for the night. Sometimes, now not always, the lad would have been so hammered the night before that when he approached Clery's clock, he would see the girl and realise she wasn't as pretty as he remembered and cross the street. I'm sure a few women have also indulged in this cruel pastime.

'Jesus, I feel like I'm Ronny Drew!' Martina says.

'Do you mean Nancy Drew?' Kevin asks.

We laugh out loud. The alcohol is kicking back into gear.

'I mean you can feel like a singer of the Dubliners if you want to, Martina…' I add. More laughs.

'Didn't he sing Seven Drunken Nights?' Paul asks.

'Or as David calls it– a normal week,' Kevin quips.

***

We fold into the pub. It's busy in the early evening. A band is sound-checking up the steps, and we find ourselves in the middle of the pub.

'Now what?' Kevin says.

'Pints?'

A black chap with a raspy voice hands me two pints of the black stuff and two ciders. Then we take in the atmosphere. In Budapest, there would always be music on in the background. It's like a central European thing. Here, in Ireland, all you have is the droning sound of chatter with a few clatters of laughter. I love it. I smell the cold pint in my hand and take a gulp.

Fucking magic. Here's to the demon.

I'm trying to think about what happened in the Foggy Dew in *Cheers! Darling*. It has been a minute since I wrote it. Why would Jenny choose this chapter out of all of them? What clue should I be looking for?

'Did anyone take the book with yiz?'

I get a volley of "No" in return.

Shite.

'Does anyone have the Kindle app on their phone?' I ask.

'You want to read the book?' Paul mumbles.

'Nobody reads anymore,' Kevin says with a smile. He likes this. I think the gamification of finding out our father was an adulterer is appealing to him.

'But you wrote it?' Paul adds.

Martina and Paul are huddled together, talking in hushed tones, when my Kindle app finally downloads. I search for *Cheers! Darling* and, grab myself a copy. By the time the next pints arrive, I'm on the Foggy Dew chapter:

> Yvonne leaned back in her chair in the corner of the bar, far from the soundchecking trad band. She swirled the deep amber liquid in her glass as she began recounting the misadventure of her date with Carl from three years ago. The soft hum of conversation and the distant melody of traditional Irish tunes provided a backdrop to her tale of woe.
>
> As she took a sip of her Captain Morgans and coke, she began, "The moment he walked in, I knew I was in for a rough ride. Carl, with his unruly mop of hair and an overabundance of charm that reeked of insincerity, strutted in like a peacock in a henhouse."
>
> Yvonne's gaze drifted to the ceiling as she recalled the cringe-worthy details. "He insisted on ordering a cocktail with an umbrella, bless his heart. In a Dublin pub! I tried to hide my horror, but Carl, oblivious as ever, started regaling me with tales of his supposed prowess in the financial world. 'I'm an entrepreneur,' he said.

My eyes flicked back to the beginning of the paragraph.

> *Yvonne's gaze drifted to the ceiling as she recalled the cringe-worthy details.*

I stood up and checked for the furthest table from the band.

'You found something?' Kevin asks.

I'm doing the dramatic thing you see in movies. You know, the part where the protagonist just ups and walks away, deep in his focused mind. I move to the end of the bar, my eyes glued to the wooden panelling on the ceiling. That's when I spot it: a taped envelope above the last table on the left.

'Everything alright?' the occupant of the table says. He's a skinny lad with salt and pepper stubble. He looks like Gollum with hair.

'I think that's my letter,' I say.

'What's it doing up there?' he says, craning his neck.

'It's a treasure hunt.'

'Treasure hunt!' he bellows, chuckling to himself. 'What's the treasure?'

'A sister, I think.'

'Yea' wha'?'

'I think there's a sister at the end of the rainbow.'

I start to negotiate my way up the stool and stretch for the taped envelope.

'Like a black woman?' the skinny man asks.

'What?' I say, nearly buckling on the flimsy stool.

'Is it like a "sista"-- a black woman? Or like a "sister"-- like a nun?'

A line appears between me eyes as I snatch the envelope. "What? No, like a sibling.'

'Ah, I have one of those,' he says. 'Don't need another. I wouldn't mind a sista though. I heard if you go black you never go back.'

'Erm, okay,' I say, ready to rejoin the brothers and sista-in-law.

'Hm– Well, enjoy your treasure hunt.'

'Thanks.'

'Why the black suit? You at a funeral or something?' he asks.

'Yeah, me da's.'

'Jaysus, I'm sorry.'

'Why? Did you know him?'

'Good one,' he says and then adds, 'Do you want something for your travels? Or troubles?'

'Uh?'

He pulls out a tiny ziplock baggie-backed with jigsaw pieces. 'Something for your travels, I said.'

'It would make the night more interesting.'

'Here,' he says, 'Take two. You'll find that sista, no problem.'

He places two LSD blotter tabs into my palm, and I pop them in my mouth. It tastes of earth and chews like rubber. Gone.

The skinny man scratches his head. 'I wouldn't have done both at once.'

'What? Why?'

'Strong shit man… Bison strong.'

'Why would you give me two then?'

'You looked sad. Not on the outside,' he says and points a tiny finger to my chest.

'Thanks, bud.'

'Good luck finding your nun.'

I watch him get off his chair and head to the exit with a cigarette in his mouth.

***

Back at the table, I hand Kevin the envelope. He raises his palms to me. 'I don't want to open it.'

'Why not?' I ask.

'There could be anything in that envelope. Anthrax or something.'

'Why would she put Anthrax in an envelope for us?'

'Where would you even get Anthrax?' Martina adds.

'I could get you Anthrax,' Paul butts in.

We all look at him, trying to decipher if he was messing with us or not.

'See?' Kevin says. 'If Paul could get some, some townie could definitely get Anthrax.'

'Fucking dicks,' I mutter and rip open the end of the envelope. There is an audible gasp from the table as I do it. 'Would yiz fuck off. There's no Anthrax in it.'

A piece of paper flops out onto my hand. It's the size of my palm, cut haphazardly into a square.

'What is it?' Martina asks.

'I think it's a piece of paper,' I say.

'Sarcasm is the lowest form of humour, David,' Kevin says.

I turn the page over. It's a homeprinted picture of our da and a small redhead girl on his lap. He's younger in the picture. Jenny must be four or five. They're sitting in a pub (typical), but I can't make out the location.

I hand it over to Kevin.

'Is there anything else on it?' Martina asks.

'No,' I say.

Kevin passes the picture on to Paul. He glances at it and passes it to Martina.

'What do we do?' she asks.

'What can we do?' I say.

'Go home?' Paul asks.

I check me watch. I would like to be home before the hallucinogens kick in. Nothing worse than freaking out in front of Kevin. 'Good idea,' I say.

Kevin looks at me, baffled. 'That's it?'

I returned the baffled look. 'What do you mean, that's it?'

'You've just given up?'

'What's there to find in a printed copy of a childhood photo of your half-sister and cheating Da?'

'There might be other clues,' he says and grabs the envelope. After a quick search, he drops it again.

'She's just fucking with us,' I say.

'Angry, I guess,' Paul says. I look at him to elaborate. 'I mean, wouldn't you be if you found out your da has this already grown-up family? And you have to stand in the back of the church?'

'She could have said something. I would have understood,' I say.

'But would yeh? Think about it. You're the angriest prick I know.'

'I would, yeah,' I tell Paul.

'You're in a retrospective now. And about twelve pints deep. Of course, you're going to say that. But think about her walking into the church and seeing the whole Dowling clan looking sombre at the top of the aisle. You'd be pissed. Pissed enough to mess with the brothers. Send them on a wild goose chase. If she's even our sister? I mean she could be lying about that. People are fucked in the head.'

I hold up the photo of me da, and Jenny on his lap.

'That could mean anything,' Paul continues. He's on a clear train of thought, and there's no stopping him. 'She could be good at Photoshop for all we know. What I'm actually trying to say is this: people get angry and do stupid things. And I wanted to apologise. I was pissed at you for asking for your money back.'

I arch my eyebrows at him. 'Erm, no I didn't.'

'Yes, you did.'

'Sorry… all I said was "My island awaits". You stormed off. Anyway, it is my fucking money.'

'David,' Kevin trying to say before Paul butts in.

'Yeah well. I was angry at you, and I'm sorry. I should have told you what I wanted it for.'

'What did you want it for?' I ask.

'Yea',' Kevin adds.

Paul leans forward like we're about to know who killed Kennedy. His words are slurring with every new breath he takes. 'Well, you know that me and Martina are childless.'

'You're pregnant?' I ask.

'No,' she says. A curtain drops over her face. The cider bubbliness is gone for a moment and is replaced with pure disappointment.

'As I was saying,' Paul stands for effect. I wish he didn't. He looks like McGregor just gave him a haymaker to the temple. 'We're childless, and the doctors say we can't conceive naturally.'

'So you want to do the IVF treatment?' Kevin says.

'Yep,' Paul says. 'But that costs money. The money I gave back to you, David.'

'Congratulations,' Kevin says.

'What are you congratulating them on?' I ask Kevin. There's a bubble in my belly, and the kettle is boiling.

'For wanting to have a child?' Kevin says. His eyes tell me to calm down. Several pints and a lost sister in, I'm far from calm. Maybe the LSD is kicking in.

'Why am I–why am I congratulating them on wanting to have a child? They live in a fucking council house in Finglas. No bank will touch them for a loan because of Paul's gambling issues. Fucking Martina there won't get a job to save her life. She left her last job in the cinema because it was too hard. In a fucking cinema. The only reason you're still not in Ma's house is because Da kicked yiz out. One fucking smart thing he did—'

'David,' Kevin pleads.

'So what will a child benefit from being born into your world? What? He'll learn how to mismanage any cash from his dad, and what? Be savvy on social media from his ma. That's not a fucking life.'

***

I'm on the ground. The wooden ceiling panels mix with white floating stars and squiggles. Paul is standing over me. His chest is rising and falling like a lion, ready for the kill. Kevin has a restrictive hand on Paul's arm. 'Let's get him up?'

'Yeah, he's not worth it,' Paul says.

Kevin reaches down for me. I grab his hand. I'm a bit wonky getting up. I stop to let the world catch up with me. That's when the raspy barman comes to the table, ready to kick us out.

'What's going on here lads?' he says.

'I bet me brother that I could dodge his punch,' I say. 'I lost.'

'Ah lads, leave it out,' the raspy man says. 'There'll be no more serving yiz now. You've had enough.'

'No problem,' Kevin says. 'I think we're done here anyway.'

The barman leans in for the near-empty glass and spots the photo. 'Ah, so you're the one on the treasure hunt.'

'What?' I say. The world has come back to me now. I gesture to the barman if I could finish me pint. He hands it to me.

'There was a young-wan in earlier saying she was doing a treasure hunt for her brothers and left the clue at the end there. She said it was like the twelve pints of Christmas, except you needed to figure out the pubs. I had a bit of a looksy meself, you know. Couldn't figure it out, so I let Google Lens do the magic for me.'

'Google wha'?' Paul says.

'Google Lens. I'm sure you're not allowed to cheat like that, are yiz? Did yeh figure out where the pub is?'

'No.'

'Do you want a hint?'

'Go on,' I say.

'Brendan Behan.'

He pisses off back behind the bar, leaving us standing around the table. I take the photo in my hand again. Of course.

'What does that mean?' Kevin asks.

'Behan was known for drinking in lots of pubs. McDaid's, The Waterloo bar and this one,' I say, placing the photo back down on the wet table. 'The Palace bar. Da's favourite pub in town.'

'This is as far as I can go with you,' Paul says.

I look at him. His eyes dead focused on me. Maybe he wasn't finished with the fight.

'It is?'

'Yeah, we're done. I can't take you anymore,' he says. He's not shouting– just deadly serious. 'You don't see the world around you anymore. Just you and the little candle you hold for your ego.'

I want to give a quippy comeback but decide to stay quiet. I have a sneaking suspicion that his right hook sped up the mushroom's process.

'You think you had it hard?' Paul says, taking a step back away from us. 'He was worse to me. "Paul? Why can't you be more like Kevin? Kevin does football. Kevin won a medal." And then you come along and it's "Paul why can't you be more like your little brother? He's amazing in school. He won an award for writing."'

'Paul–' Martina has a hand on Paul's arm. Is it to balance him or to calm him, I don't know.

'Just because you stood up to him,' Paul is slurring his words now. He won't remember this tomorrow. 'Because he beat you, you got out. I would have rathered his fists more than his words. Your bruises healed. Mine are still scabbing and whenever someone pokes fun at me at work or my own brother tells me I'm not good enough to be a dad– that scab comes off. It's never gonna heal.'

I don't know what to say. I want to hug him and tell him it's alright but I'm afraid to move. The lights above him start to sparkle. It's like there's the lamp and then a thousand tiny fairy lights around the lamp. Fuck.

'But I have Martina,' Paul says. 'She is so kind and beautiful and warm and loving and she makes up for all that shit that I get every day. I've been bullied all my life…' He takes an unsteady foot forward. Kevin steps in to hold him.

'But none of you have felt love the way that I'm feeling right now. You're lonely. Both of yiz. And I'm sorry for yeh. But this Jenny won't fill that void. Yer both shite brothers. Why would she want that?'

Martina takes his hand and guides him away from us. She turns and says, 'It would have been a good adventure though.'

She gives us a smile and takes her husband home.

We watch them go outside.

'Well shit,' Kevin says. 'I never thought he had it in him.'

'Me neither. He shouldn't be bullied at work with a right hook like that.'

'That will bruise.'

'Should we go after him?'

'Let him finish puking first.'

I follow Kevin's gaze. Paul is bent over just outside the door. Martina has a hand on his back.

***

It takes five minutes for Paul to stop puking. As soon as he's finished we come out to join them. No need to stand on display while a brother embarrasses himself.

'That's some amount of vomit,' I say.

'Fuck off,' Paul mutters.

Martina produces a bottle of water from her bag and Paul destroys its contents.

We stand there while Paul comes back to planet Earth. I think I'm leaving planet Earth. The streetlights are getting brighter. I think I see fairies blowing on the lamp. I know it's not real, but it's fucking cool looking.

Kevin slaps his chest with the back of his hand, and I'm back to reality.

'David wants to say something,' he says.

'I wanted to apologise to both of you. It wasn't fair for me to assume the worst.'

'And?' Kevin adds.

'And I'm the worst person to judge anyone. I just dropped two tabs of LSD and I think I'm gonna see God soon.'

Kevin and Paul laugh at my joke until they see my face.

'Wait, what?' Kevin says.

'That doesn't matter. What matters is that you come on this adventure with us. I need you and that right hook if we get into trouble at the end of the rainbow.'

'You took LSD?' Kevin says.

I lock eyes with Paul. He has a third eye on his forehead.

'I need you on this journey,' I say. I turn to Martina whose breath turns pink in the cold evening air. 'I need you too. I need this adventure. We need to find Jenny and tell her what a cunt Da was.'

Paul has a giggle at that. Martina looks at her shoes and smiles.

'Do you take LSD often?' Kevin says, not listening to a word I'm saying.

'It wears off quickly with me. But I took two. Let's go to erm, the Palace Bar and I'll try to puke it up.'

'Why don't you just puke here,' Kevin says.

'One Dowling DNA sample is enough for the Dublin Streets, I think,' Martina says and links arms with her husband.

We're back in action.

14

The Palace Bar stands as a timeless relic on Fleet Street. The Bar has still preserved its original décor from 1823 with very few updates. It's not the best pub in Dublin according to Google but it was a haven for literary minds, a place where the very essence of storytelling clung to the timeworn walls– the likes of Brendan Behan, Flann O'Brien, and Patrick Kavanagh gracing its tables as regulars in the past.

We get there a little after nine o'clock. It's buzzing. Always busy. Taking the route past Trinity College instead of going through Temple Bar was the best way to go. I don't think seeing so many people would be good for my state of mind. I tell my adventure crew that I have to puke up the LSD before we start looking for Jenny. They say they'll find a spot for us to have a drink.

I am tripping balls now.

I push my way into the toilets and go straight for the sink to lap water onto my face. I hold my breath with every splash. When I catch my reflection in the mirror, I'm alone. I could have sworn three people were pissing into the urinals when I walked in. I kill the faucet and listen. I can't hear a fucking thing. It's like I'm deaf, but I know I'm not because I can hear my breath. The mirror in front of me wobbles and bends. The glass ripples like water before my eyes. I can feel a pull and I'm through the mirror.

On the other side, I'm staring at myself.

Fuck! This is some strong shit.

I'm not in sync with my other self. He's washing his face while I'm staring at him.

'Trippy, isn't it?' a voice says from the cubical.

'Wha'?' I say to the cubicle door.

The voice behind the cubicle door begins to sing, '*I am he as you are he as you are me, And we are all together.*'

I can recognise that voice from a mile away. Especially when he sings. I used to have to listen to him butchering Tom Jones or the Beatles every Sunday when he had his weekly bath. To this day, *What's New PussyCat* is ruined for me. This trip is about to take a turn.

'So you actually came? I would have thought you were too much of a coward to take that trip.'

I'm staring at the cubical waiting for it to creak open like in some B-horror movie. The wheezing from behind the door unnerves me. Then there's a flush and the door unlocks.

'But you came,' he says, stepping out of the john, and stopping beside me. His face is still the same as I last saw him— waxy and gaunt. His hospital gown showing off his flabby bare ass. He takes deep, shallow breaths as his twiggy fingers reach for the taps.

'What do you want, Da?' I say.

'I just wanted to say thank you for the wonderful eulogy,' he says with a mocking laugh. 'It was beautiful…yeh fucking prick!'

I know this is not real. I'm tripping. It's actually me talking to myself. But the smell of bleach and burnt plastic lingers in my nostrils, making me think that it's real.

'Of all the toilets in all the towns in all the world, you haunt mine,' I say.

'Cute.'

'What's with the Marley routine? Are you going to show me my past? Try and help redeem a lost soul?' I say.

'You want to see the past again?' he asks, switching off the faucet. His eyes flick in my direction.

'Not particularly.'

'Good,' Da says and turns his whole body to face me. His eyes vanishing under the overhead light.

'So what now?' I say.

'What do you want to know?'

–'What?'

'You summoned me from my ashy sleep. So talk?'

–'I have nothing I want to say to you.'

'Nothing at all?'

–'Nope.'

'Not even about your sister?'

–'Half sister.'

'Minor details.'

–'Quite a big detail to leave out of our lives.'

'Would it have changed anything?'

–'I would have known about my sister–'

'--Half sister–'

–'And would have known what a cheating prick you were.'

'Ah! The moral high ground. Do you really want to stand on that altar, David?'

–'What does that mean?'

'Sure, did you not cheat on Nicole last year and blame the whole breakup on her?'

–'I wasn't married to Nicole.'

'That makes a difference?'

–'I did not sign a legal document bounding myself to one woman before the eyes of the Lord.'

'You don't even believe in God.'

'What sort of God would make you my father?'

'The smart kind. If I were any different you wouldn't be who you are.'

–'That's fucking donkey dick, and you know it. What sort of God would make you as cruel as you were.'

'The type of God that abandons the helpless.'

–'Did Ma know?'

'Did yer ma know what?'

–'Did Ma know about Jenny?'

'You'd have to ask her about that.'

–'She must have known. You couldn't keep a secret like that. Christ! You couldn't keep Christmas presents a secret.'

'Is there a point to all this, David?'

'A point to all wha'?'

'A point to this interpretation of me?'

'I'm not sure there is, Da. What if we find her? She obviously wants to be found. Why else would she be setting up this treasure hunt? What happens then? Does she tell us that she had a wonderful childhood? That you were the best dad ever. Does she tell us that she was heartbroken to find out that she wasn't the only heir to the Dowling throne? What happens when we find her? If we find her. I mean what–'

'Are you alrigh' bud?'

An older man stands at the toilet entrance. His red puffy face glows like Rudolf the reindeer.

'I'm grand,' I say, looking back on the empty space where my da was.

'Why are yeh talking to yerself?' the drunken elder says.

'I'm Tyler Durden.'

'Who?'

'Nobody reads anymore,' I say and push my way out of the toilet.

I am Jack's spaced out brain.

The crew look perplexed. There is a full stale pint and empty ones in front of them. I squeeze past several middle/upper-class suits with their ties undone, drinking Coors Lite. Their laughter is soaked in consumer privilege. An old man at the bar looks at me. He's the image of Brendan Behan. Fuck this trip.

'Are you alright?' Kevin asks.

'No.'

'D'ya wanna go home?'

'No.'

'You might need a new pint. You were gone a long time. Did you puke it up?'

'I'm coming down. I saw Da.'

'What?' Paul says.

'I saw Da. He said God made him my father so I could be who I am today.'

'A prick?' Paul says.

'Remind me not to try LSD,' Kevin adds.

I turn to the bartender and ask for another round. He turns around. It's me da, dressed in a black shirt and bow tie.

'Two the same?' Da asks.

'Go on,' I say.

I watch him as he pours the pints. His eyes are fixed as he lowers the tap with ease.

'It's a shame Kevin can't see me. Deep down he loved me… at least,' Da says.

'The bartender is Da now.'

Kevin, Paul and Martina look at the middle-aged barman with a bald head that shines like a snooker ball.

Brendan Behan gives me a wink and drowns his pint.

'Ask him what we should do here?' Kevin asks.

'Fuck off,' I say.

I look to the ceiling for help. The glow from the array of whiskey bottles above the bar begins to blind me.

'Where's your ma?' Da says, topping up the last pint. I'm trying to ignore him. Trying to look for clues like some shitty TV show that I would never watch. I'm trying not to freak out that the whiskey bottles above the bar are on fire. The smoke from the fire is slithering its way to the skylight on my left.

'That's right, she left,' Da says from behind the bar. He plops both pints down on the bar and I drop a twenty.

'That's because you can't stop giving her grief about abandoning her child,' Da the barman says. 'You're just like me.'

Keep your mouth shut David. Don't make a scene.

'We're made from the same mould,' Da says from the cash register.

I feel like I'm Jack Torrance in The Shining, haunted by ghosts at the bar. Except if he talked to the ghosts, there was no one around to tell him he'd lost his fucking mind.

'Are you sure you're okay, David?' Kevin says. When I turn my attention back to him I see the concern on his face.

'With the amount of LSD you took, you might be able to see God,' Da says, handing me back my change.

'There is no God.'

–'What's he saying?' Kevin asks.

'There's no God?' Da says. 'Then who the Fuck is tha'?'

He points to something over my shoulder. I turn around to see a muscular beast of a man decked out in animal pellets and leather fixtures. His skin is shiny with anointing oils. His beard is as wild as his one good eye. The other is hidden under an eye patch.

'I am your fucking God,' he screams in Old Norse but the LSD translates it in real-time.

I grunt and turn back to Da, replaced by the real barman.

'Are you okay?' Kevin asks. He places a firm hand on my shoulder. I can feel his pulse through his fingertips.

'I bet you can't find me!' a child says behind me. I spin around. The bar spinning with me. I spot a little red-headed girl in pigtails running between the legs of the patrons.

'Jenny?' I call out.

'C'mer Jenny,' I hear Da say somewhere in the crowd.

I stand and follow, pushing past locals enjoying a pint and a chat.

'I love you Daddy,' the young Jenny says. I can't see her yet. There are too many people in front of me.

'Sit up here on Daddy's lap,' I hear Da say.

I slide past the last drinker leading into the seated area. Da is sitting on the edge of a chair, his legs spread with Jenny on one knee. A large mirror hangs behind his head with wonderful oil portraits on either side of him. There is a flash. I see a woman taking a photo and then they are gone.

I'm left standing in front of a middle-aged woman, staring at me. She's gripping her handbag for dear life. How long was I standing there?

'Can I check under your table?' I ask.

'For what?' she says.

'Treasure.'

'Piss off.'

'I'm trying to find me sister.'

'She's not under the fucking table.'

'Can I just–' I begin to say.

'Here's me husband now. Jimmy!' she calls out. 'This fella's acting all weird.'

I turn to see a hulking man approach. He has a wild beard to match his eyes. Much like Odin from a few minutes ago.

'You fucking with my wife?' he barks in his Northside accent.

'Piss off Odin, I just want to see under the table.'

'You want to see up her skirt, is it?' the big brute says before grabbing me. I know what's coming. This will be twice in one night where I see the world from the comfort of a hardwood floor.

***

I'm looking up. Kevin is pulling on Odin's shirt. Me Da is laughing from the bar. Paul is trying to help Kevin. Martina is pointing the finger at the big man's wife. The bar staff are scrambling on red alert. I tilt me head back looking under the table where the picture was taken of me Da and Jenny. There it is. The next clue. I reach up to grab it before I'm hoisted into the air by strong arms.

15

I hit the pavement with a thud. I'll have a sore arse tomorrow.

Martina protests as she is dragged outside by a heavy-set barman.

'Jesus, will you leave it out? I've done nothing!' she bellows.

Paul calls her name from the dirty footpath. He's on my left, Kevin on my right. Kevin is already on his feet, flipping the barman off.

'Yer a bunch of pricks,' he shouts.

'Yer all barred,' the barman volleys back.

Kevin picks me up from the icy ground. 'Did Brendan Behan get barred from there?'

'I hope so,' I say as I drag myself up, leaning heavily on Kevin.

We all pause for a moment, looking at each other. Letting the adrenaline take over. Paul is the first to crack. He bursts out laughing. We follow suit.

'I'm sure yer da would have loved that you had a fight at his wake. This is fun,' Martina says.

Paul stops laughing for a moment to reflect on his wife's words. She was having fun with all of this.

'He probably would,' Paul says and gives us the biggest smile. Even now he still wants to impress the da.

'Who's hungry?' Martina asks.

'I'll only be hungry if you say the magic word to me,' Paul says.

'Supermac's?' she says.

Oh yeah…

***

We're on O'Connell Street queuing up inside a fairly busy Supermac's, considering how early into the night it is. Drunken splurges of burgers and curry chips are usually reserved for the wee hours of the morning.

Supermac's was Paul's favourite go-to fast food restaurant. If anyone ever visited Dublin you might have noticed this restaurant and thought it was a McDonald's rip-off. I'd say McDonald's might think so too. They tried suing Supermac's for the copyright of the "Mc" in the name but lost. It was a victory for small businesses over the corporate giant. Another reason not to fuck with the Irish.

Paul would remember day trips to town with me Da and Kevin. They'd always stop in Supermac's for a slice of pizza. That was their treat. It's Paul's treat now. He's at the counter ordering a slice of pepperoni and jalapeno pizza, a large Coke and chips. Martina goes for the chicken tenders, chips and a cup of tea. (It's Ireland. We get tea everywhere.)

'Next please,' the cashier says.

I order a double bacon-cheeseburger, chips and curry sauce. It's gone within seconds of sitting down. Did it snuff out the hunger? Nope. It was like the first appetiser of a tasting menu.

Paul breaks the silence of our feeding frenzy. 'So, eh, are we going home now?'

All eyes are on me.

'I mean we didn't find the next clue and I think we're barred from the Palace bar.'

I finish chewing on the last corner of me burger. The chips are long gone.

'Luckily I was cracked in the jaw. Otherwise I would have never found this..'

I plant the white envelope on the muggy table. Looking at it now in full fluorescent light. I see the name: *Paul* written on it. He cocks his head, reading it for himself.

'The fuck?' he says and opens the seal.

'Read it out loud,' Martina says.

Howaya Paul,

Hope this letter finds you in good spirits after the day's events. Hehe. I'm Jenny, your half-sister you never knew you had! Bit mad, right Anyway, I thought it was about time we got talking and figured out this family connection.

Growing up on my end was a bit of an amazing journey – dodgy haircuts, questionable fashion choices, a ghost of a daddy, a junkie mammy, moving from place to place, getting passed around for a score, the whole shebang.

Now, let's dive into the main event – you!

So, brace yourself for this one: I recently embarked on a day-long investigation into the life and times of Paul Dowling. No, not in a detective movie way, more like a curious sibling way. First stop, watching you head off to work. Office, I was guessing? But no, Jesus, a scruffy old building site in Swords. But who knows, maybe you're a secret artist or something that gets inspiration from shite construction sites?

Then, imagine my surprise when I spotted you popping into the bookies. A sly flutter on the horses, maybe? Or are you a secret expert on greyhound racing? I'm genuinely intrigued.

But wait, there's more. Lunchtime rolled around, and I was like a stealthy ninja observing your every move. What would be the Paul lunchtime special? A hearty sandwich or a gourmet salad? Do you secretly indulge in a guilty-pleasure bag of crisps? Couldn't see what you were eating. You looked up once, right at me. But I was just another face in the crowd. Not a sister.

Post-lunch, you were off to the local pub. A quick pint or a cosy corner with a cuppa? I don't know. I'm guessing a pint, because, well, Ireland. And who can blame you? Construction is hard. Just like Daddy. But you're nothing like Daddy. I saw the lads giving you stick. Called you all the names going and you just took it. Do you need your little sister to take care of it?

Anyway, I won't bore you with all the nitty-gritty details, but let's just say I've got the lowdown on your daily escapades – all in good spirits, of course.

Now, before you start thinking I've gone full-on stalker mode, I promise it's just a bit of craic. No hidden agenda, just a girl wanting to get to know her long-lost bro.

So, what do you say, Paul? Fancy a chat, maybe over a pint or a cuppa. No pressure, just a chance to swap stories and have a laugh. If you're up for it, stick with the other two. The next clue is in a hut.

Looking forward to hearing from you, and let's make up for lost time Say hello to Martina for me. Hope the whole baby thing works out.

Cheers.

Yours, Jennifer.

'What the fuck?' Kevin says.

'Did you hear that?' Martina adds. 'She was stalking you.'

'I mean, she has nice handwriting at least,' I say.

'That stuff about the baby. How would she have known unless she was following us to the hospital?' Martina says.

Paul's eyebrows join for a quick discussion before he says, 'I think we should stop. Something doesn't feel right,' he waves the letter in front of his face. 'This has just made it darker than a fucking treasure hunt.'

'Granted,' I say, 'she does come across as stalkerish. But put your hands up if you wouldn't follow your estranged half-brother around for a day to see if he is a psycho?'

I raise me hand.

'I'm being serious, David. I'm not going any further. We might end up in a plastic bag beside Da's ashes if we do,' Paul says.

'Oh, C'mon,' I say.

'Fucking pussy!' Da says.

I look behind Paul to see Da, still in his hospital dress, speaking with a mouth full of chips.

'He never had the balls to finish anything,' Da mumbles.

I thought I was coming down from the trip. Guess there are some speed bumps on the way down.

'Fine,' I say, dropping my napkin down. I shake the cup of Coke to see if there is anything left. Nothing. 'I'll go meself. I'll see it through.'

'Ah David, don't,' Martina says.

'This is crazy,' Paul says.

'I'll go with yeh,' Kevin says.

I turn to him. He nods, two soldiers out on a mission into enemy territory.

Paul drops the letter in front of me. 'Read this again,' he says. 'She's got a few screws loose.'

'Sure, don't we all,' I say.

16

We say goodbye to Paul and Martina at the taxi stand. Kevin leans in for hugs and I linger in the background. There is something I want to say now that the acid is wearing off and the crisp night air shocks me into a state of almost clarity.

I hug Martina and say, 'I think you'll make a great mammy. Forget what I said. I'm just jealous that he found someone to have kids with.'

She gives me a smile and kisses my cheek long and hard.

'Hey, hey, hey, fame fucker,' Paul says in jest. He pulls his wife off me in a playful tug-of-war.

I give him the longest hug. 'I'm sorry for your loss,' I say.

'Wha'?' he says.

'You'll make a good dad. I'll send you the money back. It's not a loan.'

'Wha'? I can't, no.'

'You can and you will.'

'Thanks, David.'

'I love you, you know that?'

'Ah-here,' Kevin says and jumps in for a cuddle.

'Ah sure, why not,' Martina says and jumps in too.

That, ladies and gentlemen, is what would have happened if this was a Richard Curtis movie. But it is not. What really went down was this:

I hug Martina and say, 'I think you'll make a great mammy. Forget what I said. I'm just jealous that he found someone to have kids with.'

She looks at me. 'Thanks for that. I know it's a lie. You shouldn't have to tell lies to people.'

'I mean it.'

'No,' she says, her thoughts wandering. 'I think you meant to say what you said in the pub. It's okay. I can't please everyone.'

She steps back and enters the taxi.

I turn to Paul and give him the longest hug. 'I'm sorry for your loss,' I say.

'Wha'?' he says.

'You'll make a good dad. I'll send you the money back. It's not a loan.'

'I knew you had a heart.'

'Sorry for what I said, about you being a dad thing.'

'No, you're not.'

We slap each other's back.

'Could you send me the money before you get murdered by a psychopath?' he asks.

I think he's messing but I'm not sure.

We wave goodbye.

***

Kevin gives up waiting for a taxi after a twenty-minute no-show at the terminal. We head on foot past the Parnell Monument and the Gate Theatre, (bastards rejected two of my plays when I was younger) and ramble up Parnell Square.

The night wraps around us like a cool, worn-out scarf as me and Kevin shuffle on past Victorian redbrick buildings. Mostly flats, I'd say. There are a few hotels. There used to be a deadly music shop that sold guitars and shit. Now it's a restaurant. The culture is dying. The street lights flicker like distant stars as we reach the top of Frederick Street where Mayes pub used to be. The sign is still there, with the cartoon lad standing on an ostrich and a seal trying to check the time on a clock. The legend above it says MAYES TIME. Now it is a fucking Centra newsagent. Another Covid victim, I bet.

Me and Kevin are shooting the shit. It's nice to have a real laugh with him. Amazing what death can do. Lift the pressure off relationships. I know it can go both ways. Our echoing laughter blends with the faint hum of the city. But as we pass by an archway on Blessington Street, a mysterious melody bounces off the walls of the alleyway and into the quiet night. We both stop, mid-step, looking at each other with raised eyebrows.

The haunting tune seems to rise from the alley and wrap around us like a mist. It takes a moment to recognise the familiar chords of "Unchained Melody" but it's not the lively rendition from the pub; it's stripped down, haunting, like the song's been soaked in bourbon.

Woahhhh, myyyy love, my darliiiing…
I've hungered for yourrrrr touch–

I'm planted to the pavement listening as the verses of the song take on a different weight, the lyrics hanging in the air with an unexpected depth. The voice of an angel is singing to me and she's hurting through her words. It's as if the night itself is adding to her pain.

'Jaysus,' I manage to say.

'He's beautiful,' Kevin mutters.

'He?'

I look again. It's hard to make out her figure in the dark but it is the voice of a woman. The smash of a bottle behind us snaps us out of our trance. I spin around to an empty street – which is fucking weird for Dublin City.

'That's our cue to leave,' I say, guiding Kevin back on track with a healthy push.

***

We turn off Blessington Street onto Berkeley Street on the long stretch to Phibsborough and The Hut Bar. On the corner of Berkeley, right outside the closed pharmacy, we stumble upon a small group of buskers, gathered in the feeble glow of a flickering streetlight. One lad, with a worn-out acoustic guitar, croons the lyrics to "Unchained Melody" that sends shivers down our spines. The other buskers both male and female, join in.

'Da fuck,' I say, knowing that the same song is unlikely to be sung twice in the space of 500 metres. There is something afoot.

The Dublin night transforming it into something raw and otherworldly. Kevin and I exchange glances.

Lonely rivers flow

To the sea, to the sea

To the open arms of the seeeaaaa, yeaaah

We press on, the haunting tune following us like a persistent ghost. The atmosphere thickens like a blanket on a cold couch. The harmonies cast a spell that's both unsettling and strangely beautiful. Why the Righteous Brothers though? Looking back, we see the buskers continue their impromptu gig, their figures blending into the night's shadows. They seem to turn to face us, willing us to come back to their siren song.

This acid trip better piss off soon. I'm getting freaked out.

17

The Hut, or Mohans of Phibsborough is a family-owned Victorian bar on the north side. It's the pub you think of when you're on Phibsborough Road. Most people would walk by it and head straight to Doyles Corner or cross the street to Bohs pub. I have never had the pleasure of darkening its doors until now. And Jesus, it's a lovely little pub. No of the hype or gimmicks you get in the heart of the city. Just an old-fashioned pub with a warm, friendly atmosphere. I mean we get a few looks when we come in but they wither away as quickly as they came.

'Jacks,' Kevin announces before disappearing behind the door to the gents.

I'm lucky to find two stools under the switched-off television. Worn wood and mirrored glass partition the bar into three small sections. I'm in the first one in front of a Guinness, Smithwicks, and Carlsberg tap. The short, bald barman takes my order. He has an air about him that makes me think he's the boss. That and he's telling the lounge girl what to do. I like how the Irish bar staff dress. Most continental Europeans dress in a T-shirt and jeans. Granted they have a logo of the bar and the whole shebang but here, in Ireland, they dress nice. These folks are in black shirts and ties with black slacks. There's a white rag tucked into his belt which gives him a hint of class that is missing elsewhere.

'It sure does.'

I stretch me neck to see who's talking. Sure it has to be James Joyce, in his dark suit, tie and hat. His round glasses make him look like an ill-placed Harry Potter. These drugs need to wear off soon.

'It sure does wha'?'

He fixes his moustache with his index and thumb.

'I believe there is a "T" in what,' he says.

'Don't talk to me about the English language,' I say. 'I had to read your books when I was younger.'

'Cute,' he says. 'So you're on a bit of an adventure. I've written about a Dublin adventure.'

'You stole it from Homer,' I say.

'If you insist on interrupting me,' Joyce growls, 'I'll piss off back to Zürich.'

'Fair enough. Who's to argue with a figment of my imagination,' I say and lean into the bar and listen.

'The thing about adventures is, they have to end. It's a journey. A lesson has to be learned. What have you learned? That you struggle with the bottle? But you'll look after that tomorrow. And maybe tomorrow you'll think of another reason to drink. Maybe tomorrow you can't write what you want and you'll think that if that Behan bastard can do it drunk and that Hemmingway bastard can do it drunk then maybe that's your niche too. Look what good it did in your last disaster of a book. Drinking your way through an all-inclusive bar with a laptop and a copy of World War Z. Your book was shite and you know it.'

'Thanks, James.'

'Mister Joyce, I've earned that respect. They have a fucking day named after me.'

–'After your character but that's neither here nor–'

'Do you want me to fucking leave without giving you the piece of advice I came here to give you? Yeh-wee-cunt-cha.'

I gesture for him to go on.

'Where was I? Weeping Jesus on the cross, you made me lose my train of thought.'

'Sorry Ja– Mister Joyce.'

'Ah yes,' Joyce says, 'Think you're escaping and run into yourself. Longest way round is the shortest way home.'

'What?' Kevin appears out of nowhere.

Mister Joyce is gone in the blink of an eye, replaced by a brother with bloodshot eyes and a sway that would give Elvis a run for his money.

'I was quoting Joyce,' I say.

'Sure didn't the great man once say, it's time to move onto shorts.'

'I'm not sure he did,' I say.

'Ah he did,' Kevin says, struggling to sit on the rustic, brown-woven high stool.

'You alright, bud?'

'The fresh air got to me.'

The barman comes back to us with the pints I ordered. I tell him I'll take them and let Kevin order a vodka and coke. He'll be dying in the morning, but sure lookit, that's what tonight is for, saying goodbye to demons and the father we never had.

'Excuse me,' I say to the lounge girl as she passes. 'Would you by any chance know if Jenny left something for her brothers here, would yeh?'

'Ah yeah. You're the ones.'

She disappears and comes back with a letter. It's for Kevin.

'Do you want me to read it for yeah?' I ask him.

'Jesus, yeah, I left me glasses at home.'

'That's why you're gee-eyed,' I say.

'Funny.'

I rip off the seal and start:

Hey Kev,

I can call you Kev, right? Got a moment to chat about a day in your life? I tagged along and watched from the sidelines. Yeah, it's weird, but I needed to see the real you. I saw you come out of your house a little after 9. Is it rented or bought? Doesn't look like you work. You started at the shops, right? Saw you navigating those aisles, picking up the essentials. Is that a vegan diet that you're on? It's mundane, but it's life, and it fascinated me – the routine of it all.

Then there was your pit stop at the house, looking after your ma. That hit a nerve, you know? I never had that. Watching you care for her, dealing with the heaviness of it all, made me wish for a connection I never had. My own ma died years ago. Died with a needle in her arm and twenty quid to her name. At least your ma has a nice house to leave you.

Kev, the real eye-opener was those rough kids on the street. The way you dodged their abuse, and stood your ground – spoke volumes. I could feel the weight of it, the struggle, and it made me wonder about the battles you fought and the scars you carry. Is it hard being gay in Finglas? They must torment you. I know I would have if I was their age again. Jesus, I was terrible.

Dublin can be a battleground, and you, my brother, are a warrior. Maybe that's why I needed to tail you, to see if we shared the same scars, the same war stories. You don't watch TV, do you? And you don't bother closing your backyard curtains. Why is that? You have weird taste in music though. I had to Shazam it to find out what it was. Sammy Davis Jr. Why do you listen to such sad songs? Mr. Bojangles. Are you the dancing clown? Or are you the one who sits on the sidelines, bobbing your head?

I get if this is too much, too weird. But if you're up for it, let's face our demons, and share our stories. If not, no hard feelings. Tell that brother of yours that if he wasn't calling people cunts he would have realised that if he followed his own book he would have found the pot of gold at the end of the treasure hunt. Yvonne from his story would have lived in the end if I had written his book.

Yours in the shadows,

Jenny.

***

Kevin sobered up without a lick of coffee or a splash of water. It's amazing what words can do. He looks at the vodka but doesn't trust his hand to hold it. I'm sure he wishes he could teleport the content into his bloodstream at this very moment.

'She was outside my house,' he says.

'Um-hmm.'

'Fuckin' staring in.'

'Yep,' I say. I'm treading carefully. Kevin looks like he's on the brink of a meltdown or an outburst. Both of which I don't want to see right now.

'When I saw her outside Ma's house, was she stalking her too?'

'It might have been the day she was stalking you.'

'Fuck…'

I think about my next words. They need to be right. Kevin's hand makes a pass for the vodka. He gets it. It's in. He's immediately drunk again.

'Should we call it quits,' I say.

It is getting a bit odd. Someone that we have never met is following us. And the scary thing is, none of us even knew she was doing it, which makes her good at it. Sure, look at the effort she made for this treasure hunt. Fuck me, I wouldn't put that much effort into a surprise birthday party. I know she's nuts but I have that itch I need to scratch even though the doctors told me not to. I need to know what's at the end of the rainbow.

'Yeah. It's getting too late in the day to be this foolish.'

'Yeah,' I say, defeated.

The big brother has made the decision.

'David,' Kevin says with a serious tone. I catch his eye. 'I want to tell you something. I want to tell you something, not because I'm drunk.'

'I know. She's dangerous. I'm getting that.'

'No, no. Not about her. Fuck her and her *my brother, the warrior*. Fuck that. Fuck her. It's you I want to talk about.'

Just over Kevin's shoulder, James Joyce raises a glass of red wine. *Cheers, darling!*

'I'm sorry for going on about the drink. I'm sorry for saying that all the time,' Kevin slurs his words now. The Vodka has anchored. 'I'm worried that there are forty to fifty books in you. Wonderful fucking stories that will never be told if you drink yerself to death. You have a talent.'

'Thanks, bud,' I say quickly to avoid a compliment. I cringe at compliments. Compliments were invented for Americans.

'Shut up and listen,' he says dismissing me. 'I read your first book…' Kevin can't think of the title. He clicks his fingers trying to find it.

'Greenroom.'

'Greenroom. What a fucking book. I was on a beach in Malaga. Fucking baking sun. I was heartbroken and cheated on. The dregs of life. And then I look at your fucking book that you sent me. My asshole brother is shoving his talent in my face.'

Maybe this isn't a compliment.

'I start reading and I'm floored. It was raw. It was true. I cried for that mother in the book. I know she wasn't our ma. But she felt like her. Because I could relate to her, as a son, as a man. Then I keep fucking reading and I see that she's trying to protect her son from the horrors of Dublin schools because she knows he's gay. Even though he didn't know it yet.'

Kevin stares at the bar as if someone switched him off. I'm a deer watching the other deer in headlights.

'Do you know, when I came ou–' Kevin pauses, fighting back the vibration of emotion trembling through his system. 'When I came out to Ma, do you know what she said?'

I shake my head.

'She said–' another longer pause. He's losing the battle with his tears. His eyes are moist. A dam ready to crack and burst.

'She said… Ah yea', sure Stevie Wonder could see that.'

I chuckle, breaking the tension. Kevin scoffs and joins in the relief.

'Thing is,' he says, wiping a tear away. 'You have a talent, and I lied. I read all your books. Every single one of them. And then I got angry at you behind your back because you write shite to pay for your next binge. Zombies in Turkey? Fuck me! I struggled with that one.'

'It wasn't me finest hour,' I say.

I take one of the pints and down it. I look at the other. I think I'm full.

'Do you have anything new?'

I don't tell him about the notes in my phone.

'No,' I say and then have a think. I almost laugh out loud. 'I might write about tonight.'

Kevin giggles. 'Some story.'

'Yeah,' I say. 'Doesn't have an ending though.'

'You're a writer. Make it up?'

'Is she a nice half-sister or an evil half-sister?' I ask.

'Jaysus, I dunno. After this letter,' Kevin says, scrunching the paper up. 'I'd say evil.'

'Yeah?'

'Yeah…'

'Jesus.'

I nod me head towards the exit. Kevin agrees. We say goodbye to the bar staff.

'C'mer,' the barman says. 'Are you that writer?'

'I am.'

'Jaysus.'

Why do they always say that?

***

Outside, like magic, a taxi is parked with its lights on. Kevin gets in the back first.

 Is she a nice half-sister or an evil half-sister?

I can't just make it up. I need to know. That itch needs to be scratched. That rainbow needs to be conquered.

I stick my head in the back.

'I need to know, Kevin,' I say. 'Love you, brother.'

He looks at me. He could be hurt, he could be drunk, he could be contemplating a shart. I can't read his expression. He nods and then tells the taxi man to head to Finglas. I swing the door shut and think of the clue in the letter: *Tell that brother of yours that if he wasn't calling people cunts he would have realised that if he followed his own book he would have found the pot of gold at the end of the treasure hunt. Yvonne from his story would have lived in the end if I had written his book.*

At the end of the book…

Fuck me. Cast your mind back to what Kevin said in O'Neill's bar. If you can't, I'll give you a refresher. *'Why not just go to the last place in the book. That's where she is, right?'*

And I say to himself: *Oh, of course she'd be at the last pub.*

I open the last chapter. John Kavanagh's: The Gravediggers.

Well, of course, she'd be in the last pub. I look down the Phibsborough Road. Sure fuck it, it's on the way home anyway.

18

I turn onto Prospect Square. The quiet little alcove on the outer walls of Glasnevin Cemetery. Red brick houses to my left, and a patch of grass between me and the Gravediggers pub.

I've gone full circle. John Kavanagh's: The Gravediggers. First pint of the day and the last pint of me life.

I cross the grass about to finish the treasure hunt once and for all. The final nail in the proverbial coffin. If my sister turns out to be a psycho stalker, so be it.

I suck in the cold, moist air. That salty Dublin air. Me body is frozen from the wrong choice of jacket. Me head feels like I've stuck it in a washing machine for a quick spin.

I close in on a group of smokers outside the bar when something catches me eye. A flicker of light in the cemetery. It gives me pause. Then I see it again, shadows on the horizon. I walk past the cloud of cigarette smoke and linger at the graveyard gates. It's a lantern. Two lanterns. Christ! There is a congregation.

My writer's brain kicks into overdrive, spinning tales of ghosts and spirits gathering in the cemetery under the cover of night, with only the moon and lanterns to guide them. My heart quickens with a mixture of excitement and trepidation as I consider the possibilities. Could it be a secret gathering of the dead, summoned by some unseen force?

Bollix.

Or perhaps a group of mourners paying their respects in the darkness, their lanterns casting eerie shadows on the gravestones?

Possibly.

Satanist ready to sacrifice a virgin at midnight?

I mean, it wouldn't be as far from reality as ghosts.

I hesitate at the gates, torn between the lure of the unknown and the confrontation of a potential sister. The flickering light beckons me closer, drawing me into the darkness of a cemetery. With a deep breath, I step through the gates and into the graveyard.

I am fucking shaking. Is it the cold or the anticipation of death? Fuck knows. I approach the figures huddled around a grave, their faces illuminated by the soft glow of the lanterns. Their whispers carry on the night breeze. I feel like I'm intruding on their private moment, but something compels me to stay, to bear witness to this hauntingly beautiful scene. Hooded cloaks and gas lanterns circle a gravestone about twenty metres from me. A chorus of chanting cuts the silence of the night.

'We gather here beneath the moon,
In this sacred space, on this hallowed ground.
With candles bright and hearts sincere,
We honour those we hold so dear.'

As I listen to the haunting chant, hairs begin to stand rigid on my forearms. I find myself drawn closer to the ensemble. Despite my initial apprehension, there's a sense of calm in the air that compels me to stay and bear witness to whatever ceremony is unfolding before me.

'Earth and air, fire and sea,
Elements guide us, set us free.
Blessings upon the departed soul,
May their spirit find peace and be whole.'

The flickering light of the lanterns casts eerie shadows across the mourners' faces, lending an otherworldly atmosphere to the scene. Faces of young and old, man and woman. The figures in their hooded cloaks move with purpose, their voices blending into a haunting melody that seems to echo through the cemetery.

'In the circle of life, in the cycle of death,
We offer our love, with every breath.
As above, so below, as within, so without,
Blessed be this soul, without a doubt.'

Their chanting keeps repeating, with a leader of the group pouring a jar of dust into the air. They chant until the group climaxes in a round of "Ahhhs."

As I stand there, watching the mourners disperse into the night, a profound sense of contrast washes over me. This pagan ritual I just witnessed feels raw and authentic compared to the scripted rituals of my Da's Christian funeral.

The day in itself flashes back to me— the sombre music chosen by my Ma, the over-rehearsed prayers, the sterile atmosphere of the church. The fake eulogy by yours truly. It felt like we were going through the motions, following a set script without truly connecting to the deeper meaning of death.

But here, in the quiet patch of the graveyard, amidst the flickering lanterns and haunting chants, there's a rawness and authenticity that resonates with me. It feels like they are not only celebrating the life of this person, but life itself. A circle of life and a circle of death. The mourners' words carried weight and depth. There was a primal connection. Natural. Spontaneous. Just like life itself. We think we go through the routine of life but a drop of rain could ruin your day.

I watch the crowd disappear into the night and decide to make my way back to the Gravediggers pub.

Suddenly, a voice calls out. 'We don't normally allow bystanders.'

I pause, turning to see a hooded figure approach with a lantern.

'Thank you for the opportunity,' I say.

'Seeing your outfit, I assumed that you were here earlier today. Am I right?' The voice was that of a woman. A well-educated woman. Probably from Howth, by the way, she said right– *Rie-sch*.

'I was…'

She drew closer. A pretty woman by the looks of her. Dark curly hair that hung down on one side of her brow. Her nose was straight as an arrow and her lips small and tight.

'A loved one, I presume. Why else would you be wandering a cemetery at night?'

'Actually, your lanterns caught my attention. What was it? Pagan?'

'Something like that. Sad really,' she said, letting the words disappear in the evening air.

'How so?'

'There are about three thousand so-called pagans left in Ireland. Not all of them tell their loved ones about their beliefs,' she says. 'Christians don't understand us. Throughout history, we have been persecuted on our own land. Forced out by a new way. We are forced to love a benevolent being and not Mother Nature herself. Tell me something, when was the last time your God did something for you?'

'That would be a tough one,' I say. I'm afraid to say I don't believe in it. Just in case she has a sacrificial dagger tucked in her cloak belt.

'When was the last time Mother Nature provided for you? Was it your breakfast, your lunch or your dinner?'

'Fair point.'

'But the Christ botherers wouldn't accept our ways. Some of us took to the sea. Some, went into hiding. Performing rituals in the dark of the night. Tonight was the funeral ceremony of a dear friend who was falsely buried as a catholic.'

'What was with the dust?' I ask.

'We dug him up last night and burned him according to our ways. Tonight we spread his ashes across his grave so that his family can still feel him when they come to visit.'

None of this makes sense to me.

'So that's you for the night so?' I ask. I'm being polite now. Not that I care. Religion, regardless which one, is all a bit much for me.

'Yes, all done for one night.'

'Lovely.'

We're walking back towards the exit of the graveyard. She holds her lantern up to my face to get a better look.

'Unless,' she says with a hint of mischief in her voice. 'You want to have some fun in the cemetery?'

'Fun?' I ask, not really wanting to know her answer.

The lantern suddenly goes out, plummeting us into darkness. The street lights in the distance turn the pagans into a silhouette. Her hand is on me crotch and she gives it a slight squeeze.

'We could have lots of fun in the dark.'

'I'm gay,' is all I could say to her. A lie but a mood killer nonetheless.

'Pity,' she says. Her voice seems far away. 'I'm tight as fuck.'

19

I push in past the gathering crowd in the Gravediggers. Do these people not have jobs that they're out this late during the week? I'm scanning their faces. Lots of young inspired people, gee-eyed and giddy. Then I spot Linda at the bar with a blonde woman. Her eyes light up for a moment. She's about to wave me over to her when I shake my head at her. I have a sister to meet. She frowns at me as I catch the barman's attention, order my last pint and head behind the frosted swing doors. Something I should have done the first time I was here.

There she is.

Jenny Kelly.

She smiles and waves at me.

'You found me,' she says.

I slump down on the stool she's pointing at. She must have been saving it all night. I picture her saying to people, "Oh, no, sorry, it's not free. I'm saving this seat for my brother."

'I found you,' I say.

'Did you like my game?'

'No.'

She looks hurt. 'Not even the part where Frank gave you two LSD tabs?'

Did she plan that?

'What the fuck? Why would you do that?'

She chuckles to herself, combing her red hair back with her fingers. 'I figured you were an intelligent person, so I needed a helping hand.'

'Hm..'

'What?' she says with a tinge of American enthusiasm. 'Aren't you happy to see your sister?'

My phone buzzes in me pocket. I look down at it. Linda's name is flashing on the screen.

'Why would you drug me?'

'It's all fun and games. Sure, you celebrity types must love the drugs.'

My phone vibrates. I glance at it.

Linda: Answer the phone!

'That's a fucked up thing to do, Jenny,' I say.

Her enthusiastic face drops to a resting bitch face. 'Sorry,' she says. 'I thought you would think it was fun.'

'Being haunted by me dead Da is not fun at all.'

I look across the room. An old man raises a drink in my direction. *Cheers*! As he lowers it I catch a glimpse of me Da's face, all swollen and bloated. A sick man's face. Those fucking drugs won't leave me system.

'I said, sorry,' she snaps.

My phone rings again. I see the blond that was with Linda pass me. She raises her baby finger and thumb up to her face, mouthing the word: *Call.*

This pins a red flag in my head. What was so important? I look at the phone. I know it's Linda but I want to make sure.

'This is not how I expected this to go,' Jenny says.

'How did you expect it to go? I want to hear the Hallmark version.'

'Hallmark does romantic Christmas films,' she adds.

'Disney then,' I correct myself.

'I was expecting a bit more enthusiasm.'

'Why?'

'Wha'chamean?'

'Why would I be enthusiastic about knowing my father was an adulterer.'

Me phone buzzes again.

'Can we start again?' Jenny asks, flustered.

'No.'

'We won't get anywhere unless–' she starts. 'Just answer the fucking phone.'

Jenny is deflated. Her cheeks flush with crimson.

I answer the phone, 'Listen, Linda, I'm having a weird night. I don't think er…'

'Yeah, that's why I'm calling yea',' she says through the receiver. 'I had this weird conversation with that woman you're talking to.'

'Oh yeah?' I say trying to sound enthusiastic.

'Yeah, she's been here since we left the Botanic House. Before you continue talking to her. As a friend, I need to tell you something.'

Is she going to tell me that she has feelings for me? I don't have the brain capacity to reject her tonight.

'I was talking to that girl earlier and your name came up. Then she got really interested and wanted to know everything about you. A real fangirl-like. She wanted to know about your childhood and our relationship. Real personal stuff. Then she says something weird. She says: "I'm related to David Dowling". But I know that's not true.'

'Um hm.'

Linda goes quiet on the other end.

I'm trying to make this sound like I'm not talking about Jenny because I have a feeling in the pit of me stomach that something is not right.

'And how do you know?' I pause to let Linda talk.

'She said that she's all alone now that her dad is dead and her Ma died a few years ago, right? Then she says that she wants to meet her new family, the Dowlings and her famous brother, but that's not all.'

'What?'

'So when I managed to get away from her, Aoife, me friend here asked why I was talking to Jenny Kelly. Aoife says yeah Jenny's a regular head-the-ball. I tell Aoife what she said to me Aoife says, "Sure, her Ma and Da are not dead. I had a drink with them last week...".'

I stop in my tracks.

Not dead?

'Wha'?'

'That's what Aoife said.'

I'm beginning to boil. It's all been a fucking lie. I look at Jenny. She sips her whiskey and pretends that she's not listening to me. I look down at the table and spot a large envelope. My mind casts back to an earlier conversation. It could be anthrax. We laughed at that thought back then. Now, I'm not so sure.

'Right,' I say. 'Sure I'll talk to you later, yeah.'

'Be careful, David. She seems like those crazy fans I see on TikTok.'

'Bye now.'

I hang up.

'All good?' Jenny says.

Her eyes are fixed on me. Her whole mannerisms change before my eyes. She went from being a strange, potential half-sister to a crazy person. Her eyes are more wild to me now. Her unkempt hair is not a fashion choice anymore. It's a lack of hygiene.

'So I was thinking, maybe we can go out for dinner with your brothers. I mean, our brothers. What do you think?'

'Not my mother?'

My mind goes to Ma. What happened when Jenny went to the house? Did Ma see through her? Did she fall for it too?

'I mean, your Mam can come too, I guess.'

'--You're not me sister,' I interrupt.

There is a pause. The splattering of chatter engulfs us for the longest of moments.

'Wha'?' she mutters.

She drops her eyes to the envelope on the table. The anthrax envelope. When her gaze returns to me the mood has changed. She is no longer the enthusiastic fake sister. Her demeanour has shifted to the defensive.

'Let me tell you a story,' she says.

'I'm dying to hear it. Is it the one where you stalk my brothers and pester my mother?'

'Why are you being such a dick about this.'

'Because Aoife at the bar knows you and knows your living parents. She had drinks with them last week.'

'Aoife at the bar, what Aoife at the bar?'

'It doesn't matter, what matters is that you haven't been entirely honest in your wicked game, have you.'

Great! Now the Chris Isaak song is triggered in the back of my head.

'You have until I finish me pint,' I say. 'No more, no less.'

She watches as I take a huge gulp from me Guinness. I split the harp and wipe me lip.

'Listen here,' she says. 'I don't give a fuck if you believe me or not, Mister Writer.'

Chris Isaak's voice is replaced by Kelly Jones from Stereophonics: *Mister Writer, why don't you tell it like it really is…*

'Yes, I have living parents. I was adopted.'

This is an angle I wasn't expecting. I lean back on my stool, cross my arms and listen to the rest of her argument.

'About a year ago, my adoptive mother found a lump in her armpit. Scared her. Scared me. She went through chemotherapy and came out the other side on top. But it triggered something in me. I thought I was going to lose another mother. That safety net, you know. My real mother was an addict. Died doing the thing she loved, I guess.'

She took a swig of her whiskey before continuing.

'I never knew my father… real father. All I had was this photograph.'

She opens the envelope and slides the same photograph she used in the treasure hunt across to me. The one from the Palace bar. My Da grinning like an idiot with Jenny on his lap. If that is Jenny. I mean. It does look like her now that I have someone to compare it to.

'I vaguely remember that day. Sitting in the pub, drinking red lemonade. I couldn't remember his face, only my mum saying that he was my Daddy. The rest is a blur.'

She drives her hand into the envelope and pulls out a certificate.

'His name is on my birth certificate.'

She slides the cert over to me. Sure enough, his name was there. "*B. Dowling.*" Not Brian. Just "*B*".

'It took me a long time to track him down. When I did, he was already in the hospital.'

I took another sip of stout. Letting her know her time is running out.

'May, your mam, was understanding,' she said. 'She invited me in for a cuppa tea and listened to my story. But when I asked if I could see my real dad, she said no. It would add stress to an already stressful situation but she would tell him that I called around.'

I doubt she did. Why would she believe a stranger out of nowhere?

'I didn't believe her so I went to visit him without her consent. I told the nurse I was family and sat with him while he slept. I shat myself thinking that one of you would walk in and catch me,' she said, taking her own sip to calm her nerves. 'Then he woke up.'

I can imagine my Da waking up saying, "Who the fuck are you?"

'It took him a minute but he recognised me,' she says.

I doubt that.

'I felt this anger building up in me when he did. I don't know why. If he didn't know me then I would have excused his lack of, I dunno… Lack of interest in me? But he did recognise me. I started crying, like.'

She's starting to get upset thinking about it.

'And you know what he tells me. He said he couldn't have been my father because he had a family of his own. As if that was an excuse.'

'I mean he was barely a father to us boys,' I say.

'But he was present.'

Thinking of the years of abuse, I wonder if Jenny got off lightly.

'What do you want, Jenny?'

This stops her, mid-sip. 'I mean, whaddayamean?'

'What do you want?' I draw a line, mid-air and say: 'What is your end goal here?'

'My end goal?' she says. She looks perplexed. I'm hitting a nerve.

'What is your five-year plan?'

I watch as Jenny's face crumbles in on itself. Her chest quickens and her face becomes flush. 'Why are you saying this to me?'

'My father died with nothing. The money he has in his bank belongs to my mother. The house she lives in belongs to her children after she dies. "Her" children.'

'You think it's about money?'

'I lie for a living, Jenny. I've never done all the things I wrote about,' I begin, and pull out the letters she wrote to the brothers. I quote her lines to her; '...*saw you come out of your house a little after 9. Is it rented or bought? Doesn't look like you work.*'

I flick to the other letter addressed to Paul.

'*First stop, watching you head off to work. Office, I was guessing? But no, Jesus, a scruffy old building site in Swords. But who knows, maybe you're a secret artist or something…*'

I drop the letters, letting them float to the table. One of them tips over and falls to me lap. I watch Jenny look at the letters and not at my blank expression. There is nothing sinister about her now. Nothing is hidden in the corners of her face.

'You make a reference to money twice. Just come out and say it. See…'

I reach across and take her birth certificate. Jenny flinches, not expecting it. I look at it again and smile.

'If I wanted to tell you that I was your brother. I would just say it and it would be up to you to believe it or not. We'd have to talk again, you know. Maybe go get our DNA tested with one of those kits… We'll still do that just so I'm sure that I'm right,' I say.

I shake the certificate and notice how crisp the paper is.

'But you came prepared. You came with the agenda to have a definite answer tonight. See, this is the part in the story where Sherlock Holmes explains all the things you did wrong. Number one, nobody lets you write your initials on the birth certificate anymore. That's something you only see when you trace your ancestors. You found a B. Dowling. Good for you but, the handwriting doesn't match the rest of the form. It's slight, but a very good attempt.'

Jenny opens her mouth to speak but I continue.

'Secondly, you have me father's occupation down as "Bus Driver". Something I wouldn't have noticed in just a glance, as you intended. My father was a labourer all his life. You wouldn't know that because you didn't know him. I'm betting your actual Da was a bus driver.'

I give her a death stare, hoping to find a glimmer of guilt on her face. I don't.

'I have to say, that facade you built to hide the fact you're lying is holding up so well.'

She looks to the floor for a split second. Enough to drop that facade.

It was all a charade. This whole thing. My stomach drops and my palms flood with sweat. I've been had. Me and me family.

'Do you know how disgusting that is? On the day of me father's funeral, to do something like that,' I say.

She looks away again.

Caught.

I have her now.

'What went through your head to think that you could get away with this. Of all days.'

I lean back on me stool, trying to process the whirlwind of emotions. Me hands are shaking. I'm on a cliff with vertigo. Me stomach waves and crashes. Jenny sits across from me, her expression unreadable, her eyes darting around as if searching for an escape route. But there's no way out for her now. I test me voice for cracks.

'Answer me, Jenny,' I demand, my voice holding — for now. 'What made you think you could pull off this farce?'

She swallows hard, her hands fidgeting with the edge of the table. Like a five-year-old, caught red-handed with her hand in her Ma's purse. 'I... I don't know,' she stammers, her voice trembling slightly. 'I thought... I thought maybe... I could find a connection.'

'A connection?' I repeat incredulously. 'By deceiving me and me family? By pretending to be something you're not?'

She shrinks under my gaze, that facade she built tumbling like a house of cards. 'I just wanted... I wanted to belong to your family,' she whispers, her voice barely audible over the din of the bar.

'You have a fucking family!' I spit venom. 'Answer me this. Truthfully. Is your Ma dead? Did she die with a needle in her arm?'

Jenny doesn't answer.

'Is your Da dead?'

Nothing.

'Is your Ma dead? Is your Da dead? Answer me.'

Jenny shakes her head, her eyes glistening with unshed tears. 'I know it was wrong... I know I messed up. But I was desperate, David. I didn't know what else to do.'

'Desperate for what? Me family is in bits. Why would you want to be a part of that?'

'Because you're in it.'

Oh shit.

Why didn't I see this coming?

'I have read all of your books. Multiple times.'

Ah shit....

'I follow you on social media. I feel like we like the same things, you know?'

Sweet weeping Jesus on the cross.

'You like history, I like history. You like holidays. I love holidays. You love books.'

'Jenny. Stop...'

I hold me hands out, sweaty palms facing her. It's me looking for the exit now. I need to get away from Annie Wilkes here before she chops me leg off with an axe.

'What are you doing?' I say.

There is a moment. A wisp of air swishes across her face and I can see a change in her. Maybe it was the fact that she said it out loud, or maybe a dollop of common sense dropped on her, but she looked defeated and embarrassed all at once.

'I am so sorry,' Jenny says. 'I was desperate to meet you at first, and then–' she does this twirling motion beside her head. 'I get– I get confused sometimes. My active imagination just drives away and leaves me in the back seat for a while.'

She gathers her things in an effort to leave.

I sigh, running a hand through my hair in frustration. 'That doesn't excuse what you did,' I say firmly. 'You hurt a lot of people today, Jenny. My family, me... We trusted what you said was true, and you betrayed that trust.'

She ducks her head, shame washing over her features like a shadow. 'I know,' she murmurs, her voice barely audible. 'I'm sorry, David. I'm so, so sorry.'

'I don't think we should see each other ever again…Not me, not my family. Let's leave it at that and not involve the Guards.'

I study her for a moment, taking in the turmoil etched across her face. Despite everything, I can't help but feel a pang of sympathy for her. She's just another lost soul searching for her place in the world. A casualty of misdiagnosis. Dangerous? I'm not sure. Maybe to herself.

'Listen,' I say finally, my tone is softer than before. 'I don't know what you're wrestling with, Jenny, but this isn't the way to deal with it. Lying and deceiving others will only lead to more pain and heartache.'

She looks up at me, her eyes wide with a mix of hope and fear. 'What should I do?' she asks, her voice barely a whisper.

I pause, considering my words carefully. 'Start by being honest,' I say gently. 'With yourself and with others. And if you need help, seek it out. There are people who care about you, Jenny. People who want to see you happy and whole. I'm including myself in that. Be happy Jenny.'

She nods slowly, tears brimming in her eyes. 'Thank you, David,' she says softly. 'For forgiving me.'

I haven't fucking forgiven you, ya nut. I just don't want you to cause a scene in the pub. So I offer her a small, sad smile.

She nods, wiping away a stray tear with the back of her hand. 'I'll do better, I promise,' she whispers.

She stands to leave.

'One more thing,' I say as the memory of the postcard in me Da's coffin pops into me head. The one that said, "I'm glad you're dead."

'Did you visit me da's coffin yesterday?'

Jenny shakes her head. It could be the truth.

I watch her leave. Disappearing in the crowd like a lone sailor, lost to the sea.

20

The lights flash for the last orders. I'm nursing my pint when I feel someone slide onto the stool beside me. I glance up and there she is, Linda, with drinks for both of us.

'Mind if I join you?' she asks, her voice soft.

'Not at all,' I reply.

"Last orders," Linda says, handing me a fresh pint.

"Thanks," I mutter, taking the drink from her.

'Did you get it sorted with Jenny?'

'Yeah,' I say. I almost burst out with laughter thinking of the absurdity of the whole situation.

'And?' she says, a flash of intrigue runs across her face.

'Ugh,' I scoff. 'Maybe another day. Let's just enjoy a pint.'

I smile at her and we clink glasses.

'Where is your friend?' I ask.

'Aoife? She left. She has work tomorrow.'

'Poor her.'

'Yep. I'm jelly. Would love a bit of work,' she agrees, taking a sip of her drink. 'But I'm glad I ran into you again.'

'Me too,' I nod, taking another sip. 'You're not working at the moment?'

'Baby leave.'

She looks off into the distance of her mind. I study her face as she does. I remember the times when we were young. I would stare at her all the time, examining her face like an artist studies a model. She is still so beautiful.

Then she surprises me with her next question. 'David, do you ever wonder… what could have been?'

I look at her, caught off guard a little . 'What do you mean?'

'If things had been different,' she explains, 'If you didn't leave and we had stayed together.'

I take a moment to consider her question before answering. 'Yeah, sometimes I do.'

'Like when?'

'Like now.'

Her face returns to face mine.

'What do you think would have happened?' she asks, her eyes searching mine.

'I think…' I start searching for the right words. 'I think we would've been happy… Maybe. You never know with these things. Maybe me snoring would push you over the edge.'

She giggles. 'Maybe.'

'We had something special, didn't we?'

Linda smiles. There is a hint of sadness in her eyes. 'Yeah, we did. We were solid.'

'Until we weren't.'

'Until the hospital,' she says. Her eyes leave me again.

'If I hadn't gone to the hospital, maybe we would've gotten married,' I say, feeling a little bolder. 'Had a couple of kids of our own.'

She nods, 'Yeah, maybe,' her voice trailing off.

'And we would've lived in a cosy little house somewhere where we could afford it," I say, picturing it in my mind. 'With a shitty garden out back because me thumbs are not at all green.'

'That sounds nice,' she murmurs, her gaze drifting back for a moment.

'It does,' I agree, 'It sounds perfect.'

We sit in silence for a moment, lost in my own little fantasy. But then Linda speaks up again, her voice barely above a whisper.

'But that's not how things turned out, is it?'

I shake me head, feeling a pang of regret. 'No, it's not.'

'You wouldn't be you if you had stayed.'

'I wouldn't be me?'

'You wouldn't be David Dowling,' she turns to face me. Her posture changes. She comes on as more dominant. 'See we would have fumbled through our teens and into our twenties. We would have still tried the college scene. I would've gotten pregnant, and you'd have found a job to support us because that's the type of person I know you are. You would've dropped your dreams for me without asking.'

It's my turn to break eye contact. She's not wrong.

'Yeah, okay, we'd find a house and settle down but we'd be living hand to mouth every month.'

I take a moment to let her words sink in. Linda always had a way of cutting straight to the heart of things, even when it was uncomfortable.

'Maybe,' I concede, taking a sip of me pint. 'But who's to say we wouldn't have made it work?'

She shrugs, a hint of frustration in her voice. 'Maybe. But maybe we wouldn't have been happy. Maybe we would have resented each other for the life we could have had. We woud've turned into our parents.'

That hits home. 'Maybe,' I repeat softly. 'But that's all in the past now. A story never told. It just sits in our minds, fading like ice on a summer's day.'

'Nice,' she says, mocking me.

'I'm a writer.'

Linda nods, taking a deep breath. 'It was a nice dream.'

'But we always have to wake up.'

Linda takes a sip of her pint. A long, drawn-out sip before saying, 'Can't sleep forever.'

We then sit in silence for a moment, the weight of our history sitting on our chest, willing us to tap out

'I have one question,' I say. 'Why Paddy Cullen?'

Linda smirks on the left side of her face.

'He's a kind man.'

'He's a cunt with a capital C.'

Linda's smirk fades. I try to recover.

'Every man would be a cunt if he was dating you. Every man except me.'

She scoffs and chuckles. 'Yeah. I guess so.'

I smile, relieved to have lightened the mood. The tension between us eases, and for a moment, it feels like we're just two old friends sharing a pint and reminiscing about the absurdities of life.

'Remember that time we tried cooking together?' I say, breaking the silence.

Linda laughs, the sound familiar and comforting. 'Ah Jaysus, how could I forget? We almost burned down me kitchen trying to make spaghetti.'

'Fucking clueless,' I chuckle. 'Core memory.'

'Yeah, it is," she agrees, her eyes sparkling with the memories.

'I was able to cook with a Michelin-star chef a few years ago.'

'Ah yeah?'

'I almost burned his kitchen down too.'

The laughter comes easily, and for a brief moment, it feels like we're transported back to a time when life was simpler.

***

We head out into the night heading towards the taxi rank. Linda pulls her jacket in tight as the crisp Irish breeze attacks us for being out too late. I'm fucking freezing but try to be manly around the ex.

'You know,' Linda says, breaking the comfortable silence, 'despite everything, I'm glad we had this chance to catch up. It's been too long.'

'Yeah,' I nod, a genuine smile spreading across me face. 'Me too. It's been a strange day, but this… this was unexpected and good.'

'Yeah,' Linda agrees, wrapping her scarf tighter around her neck. 'Sometimes the unexpected is exactly what you need.'

We reach the taxi rank. Not a car in sight.

'Ah Jaysus, we'll be here all night,' she says.

As Linda turns to face me, her eyes meet mine, and in that moment, I feel an overwhelming surge of emotion. Without hesitation, I reach out and gently cup her cheek, my thumb brushing against her soft skin.

'David…' she begins.

But I don't let her finish. Leaning in slowly, I close the distance between us until our lips meet in a soft, tender kiss. It's like everything else fades away – the cold night air, the empty streets, the passing cars – and all that exists in this moment is the warmth of her lips against mine.

For a moment, we simply stand there, lost in the sweetness of the kiss. And in that brief moment, I'm alive. That emptiness that has been sitting in my stomach has been filled. I want it to wash over me.

When we finally pull away, our breaths mingling in the chilly air, I can see the surprise in Linda's eyes. But there's something else there too – a spark of recognition, of longing, of something unspoken between us.

'That was unexpected,' she murmurs.

"Yeah," I reply, unable to tear me gaze away from her. 'Sometimes the unexpected is exactly what you need.'

Lights cut across us. The yellow taxi sign on the car flicks on.

'I'll get the next one,' I say.

Linda smiles, sliding into the backseat of the cab. She touches her lips with her fingers and wriggles them at me to say goodbye.

Until next time, I almost say, but don't. There is no sign of another taxi so I walk.

It's a nice night for a walk.

21

I slide the keys into the lock and feel the door give way. It's dead quiet here. Outside, the morning birds have not yet woken to search for worms. In a couple of hours, though, they'll be singing god-awful songs while they do it.

I don't have a sister. I have a deranged fan though. The lengths that people will go to if unchecked by someone sane.

At least now I have a wicked idea for a book! I'd have to change me super fan's name to something else. I pick Jenny because sounds like a nice fake name. Jenny Kelly. Done.

I contemplate how to start it as I open the back door to have a smoke. I drift away to that kiss with Linda. As I spark one up and think about those horrid Hallmark movies – the guy finding feelings for the wrong woman – Linda. The guy is just looking for love – just like me. Except I was looking for paternal love. Jesus, I think this book could be an anti-Hallmark movie. The one that, if it was turned into a movie, would be the anti-Christmas movie. Instead of *It's A Wonderful Life,* my version of Christmas would be: *It's A Horrendous Existence.*

I actually don't think I've ever seen a Hallmark movie, so I could be getting this all wrong.

'That must have been some wake?' Ma says from the kitchen door. I give her a sideward glance, trying not to smoke inside the house.

'Aw stop!' I say. 'He's well dead now.'

She's in her housecoat and fluffy slippers switching on the kettle.

'Tea?'

There is always time for tea in an Irish household. Even if it's 01:26 in the morning.

'Nah, it's bad for me,' I say.

'Grand.'

There's silence in the air again. The street dogs are on the prowl singing Tom Waits songs. There are two of them out there, one of them in the distance, one close to home.

'So we found a sister.' I say.

I take another drag and wait for her to respond.

'Jaysus, that feckin' nut.' Ma says.

I kill the smoke and step back into the house.

'Jesus,' Ma says, looking at me black eye. 'What happened to your face?'

I forgot about that. I think the drugs and drink numbed the pain for a while. Now the darkness is coming out.

'One or two fights.'

'Are the boys alright?'

'Don't worry, Ma. I looked after them,' I say with a cheeky smile. I don't tell her that one of her boys gave me a wallop.

She pours out her hot water and stirs the tea bag as I plant me arse on a chair.

'Some journey,' I say. 'Did she really come to the house?'

'Yeah,' she says. 'She knocked on my door one day out of the blue. This was when your dad was first sent to the hospital.'

'What was your reaction when she said she was your husband's daughter?'

'What do you think? – Angry at first, then some of her stories didn't quite match up. I kept me mouth shut and played along. Told her not to visit him in the hospital.'

'Do you think she did?'

'She might have. I can picture her at his bedside saying that she's his daughter. I can see him playing along, not really knowing if it was true or not.'

'Whaddaya mean?'

Ma sits with her tea.

'Sure your father messed around. I knew it. I could smell the women off him when he came home from wherever he was. Would it surprise me if he had bastards roaming around…No.'

'Jesus. It doesn't stop, does it? So much destruction from one man.'

'Speaking of destruction, did you sort everything out with yer brothers?'

'Yeah, I think so. Kevin likes me again. Paul wants to have a kid.'

'Jesus,' she says and blesses herself. I'm not sure if it's for a grandchild or not.

I shift in my chair. It's hard and I'm tired and sore.

'One more question Ma before I head to the land of nod.'

'Go on–'

'Did you write the postcard?'

'Postcard?'

'You know what I mean. "I'm glad you're dead".'

She reaches a hand out for mine. I give it.

'Son,' she starts, then searches deep for the next few words. 'You asked me if I was relieved that he died. Now that all that madness is done I can tell you this: I loved that man. I held the world up for him. I cherished the ground he walked on… and then I married him. When you're young, you think that the love you feel in that moment will last an eternity. You think that you'll laugh at the same jokes and have the same opinion but in reality, unless you work on it, someone is going to get bored and clock out of the relationship. Your father felt trapped in his marriage. To him we held him back – the selfish prick. But in reality, we were the trapped ones. And when it reached the crescendo of violence, I knew then that it would be the norm. I ignored it, of course. "He'd never do that again", I kept saying to myself. "Surely he wouldn't hit me again". But then he did. Again and again. Letting his anger out on me… I let him because I loved him.'

I'm holding back the tears as much as I can, fighting back the urge to bawl like a baby by swallowing it.

'Then he started to release his frustration on you boys, and I realised I was helpless.'

'You weren't helpless, Ma,' my voice breaks on "helpless".

'You stood up for me, and he beat you,' her voice is breaking too. 'And I couldn't have that anymore. You were so smart. I didn't want to see you under the ground because you wouldn't stop until he stopped. You would have let him kill yeh out of spite because you'd never back down. That's when I knew I had to let you go. And I did.'

Ma starts sobbing now.

'I don't regret it, David. I don't. I look at you, and I see what you've become. Forget the local fame and the money. Look at what your brain can do. Not many people have that discipline. The only thing I missed back then was sharing space with you. That's all I ever wanted. It's all I ever want.'

I wipe a tear away from the corner of my eye.

'And yes, I am relieved that he's dead. So I wrote a note for him to read while he was in the coffin, burning in damnation. It's just a shame me life is coming to an end when it's just beginning.'

'Sure, it's the twenty-first century, you might find a rich twenty-something who's mad into cougars.'

'What's a cougar?'

She gives me a half smile. She fucking knows what a cougar is. I massage my tired face and stand. It's time to sleep.

'She is fucking nuts though,' I say.

'Who?'

'Jenny'

'You said it.'

'Something sad about her too.'

'Ah yeh,' Ma says.

Ah yeh.

END

EPILOGUE

There you have it. Six weeks of solid first draft and three weeks of rewrites. I'm actually sitting, adding the final touches here and there. Few opinions. A few jokes. Did you laugh? Probably not. People don't laugh at books anymore. People don't read. That makes you a minority. Welcome to the club.

A lot has happened in the last couple of months. I'm back home in Budapest writing this Odyssey (see what I did there?). She's a wee short book, but hopefully I've filled it with truth and heart.

Kevin has found a boyfriend. A fella named Kian with a "K" from London. They met at the Pride Parade Organisation Office at the North Dublin section's Christmas party. I noticed the wonderful taxi driver who picked me up from the airport in one of the photographs. She has a warm heart and a warmer hug.

Paul and Martina are expecting. No IVF treatment was needed. I did the math and they banged on the night of me da's wake. Dirtbags. Paul bought me a kitchen island out of the money I gave him. It was delivered last week… and now I've no fucking room in me kitchen. Fucking terrible idea. I keep bumping into shit.

Ma is doing fine. She is going on a cruise this summer to the Bahamas. She won't say who she's going with but it's none of my business. I talk to her every Friday for a chat and a rant. She says the house is too quiet for her. She might sell it and move to Sligo.

Linda sent me a drunk text one night over Christmas asking if she has beautiful eyes. This was followed by a picture of her hammered drunk. Her eyes were bloodshot. Paddy Cullen was in the background. I never answered back.

I also have not heard from Jenny Kelly since that night. I suspect I never will. Maybe she'll show up at a book reading when I go to Dublin in the Summer. Maybe not. Who cares? In the wild world of fandom, there's a thin line between being a dedicated admirer and straight-up crossing into someone's personal bubble. Jenny did that. I mean, who doesn't love a good fanbase? Who doesn't love hearing: "David Dowling, the writer… Jaysus". It's all about sharing the love for your favourite artist, actor, writer, or whatever rocks your boat. But let's be real, there's this breed of fans who take it to a whole new level, and it's not all rainbows and unicorns.

As for me. I've been 63 days sober as of today, when writing this. I have a counsellor Zoom meeting every Tuesday and a sponsor meeting every time I feel like slipping. I'm sleeping better. I'm thinking more clearly. I'm reflecting and I don't miss Guinness… that much.

That might be a lie.

Anyway, for those of you who can read: Thank you for getting this far. I've enjoyed the journey from Troy to Ithaca via the Palace Bar. Not all of this is true but it's based on a true story. Sure, don't they say, never let the truth get in the way of a good story?

Until the next time!

Keep reading,

David Dowling.

AFTERWARD

All journeys have a beginning, middle, and end, and I am filled with a deep sense of gratitude and reflection as this chapter in my life is now in your hands, whether in physical or digital form. Writing this book has been both a challenging and rewarding experience, and I am deeply grateful for the opportunity to share it with you, the reader.

First and foremost, I want to thank you for taking the time to read this book. Whether you stumbled upon it by chance or sought it out with intent, your engagement with these pages means the world to me. It is your curiosity and willingness to explore new ideas that make writing worthwhile.

I owe a debt of gratitude to those who supported me along the way. To Elaine, Katrina, Tanja and Sarah, thank you for reading and providing your first opinions on the manuscript.

I also want to extend my appreciation to my editor and publishing team. Your keen insights, meticulous attention to detail, and relentless pursuit of excellence have significantly elevated this work. Your contributions are deeply valued, and I am fortunate to have collaborated with such talented professionals.

Writing this book has been a journey of discovery. After losing both of my parents close together, I had the idea of exorcising some of the ghosts that lingered after their passing. Although this is a fictional story, I believe we can all find pieces of ourselves in the characters—whether it is wit, pain, sadness, or the inability to say sorry.

As you close this book, remember that you didn't choose your family; they were chosen for you. While you might drift apart, I hope they will always be there to listen on the other end of the phone... Unless they're cunts. In that case, just remember that you didn't choose them. Your parents did.

Thank you for being a part of this journey. I look forward to continuing this conversation with you in the future, whether through the written word or other means.

With gratitude,

Chris Slevin

Printed in Poland
by Amazon Fulfillment
Poland Sp. z o.o., Wrocław